THE ART OF POWER

The ART *of* POWER

Thich Nhat Hanh

HarperOne
An Imprint of HarperCollins*Publishers*

HarperOne

FIRST HARPERCOLLINS PAPERBACK EDITION PUBLISHED IN 2008

Designed by Joseph Rutt

Library of Congress Cataloging-in-Publication Data

Nhát Hanh, Thích.
The art of power / Thich Nhat Hanh. — 1st ed.
p. cm.
1. Spiritual life—Buddhism. 2. Buddhism—Doctrines. I. Title.
BQ9800.T5392N45425   2007
294.3'444—dc22
2007019425
ISBN 978–0–06–124236–6

08 09 10 11 12 RRD(H) 10 9 8 7 6 5 4 3

Contents

Foreword

In January 2001, I was privileged to accompany Thich Nhat Hanh and his longtime assistant, Sister Chan Khong, to the World Economic Conference, held each year in Davos, Switzerland. Thich Nhat Hanh had been invited along with other prominent religious leaders from around the planet to meet and discuss how spiritual values could be used to help resolve global issues.

Before an estimated thirty heads of state, two hundred of the world's richest men and women, and a few thousand of the most influential movers and shakers alive, Thich Nhat Hanh spoke with love, compassion, and total fearlessness. He was not there to seek support or approval from the great and famous. He was there hoping to awaken in them their best, to help them change the world by touching their own true selves. In a gathering dedicated to wealth, influence, and power in all its fabulous manifestations, he spoke in a soft and quiet voice.

He asked nothing of them, only reminding them to please always remember their common humanity. On its Web site, the World Economic Forum proudly displays the motto "Committed to Improving the State of the World." That day, in Davos, Switzerland, Thich Nhat Hanh asked everyone to adopt the motto "Committed to Improving the State of Every Heart."

Thich Nhat Hanh has spent his life speaking truth to power and truth to the powerless. He is a determined revolutionary—not one who asks us to mount the ramparts in anger, but rather a revolutionary of the human spirit, a revolutionary of understanding and of love. Born in 1926, he grew up in Vietnam, one of the most war-torn countries of the twentieth century. At age sixteen he was ordained as a Buddhist monk. From the beginning he was that rare person who could undertake multiple vocations and excel at all of them. Simultaneously he was a Buddhist monk, scholar, poet, writer, reformer, and social activist. And he did all of this as a young man in a time and place of immeasurable turmoil and suffering. He lived through the invasion of his homeland by the Japanese in 1941, the return of the French at the end of the Second World War, the guerilla war that followed and became what is known in Vietnam as the American war and in the United States as the Vietnam War. As a reformer and activist, he helped found many groundbreaking institutions, including the An Quang Buddhist Institute, which became one of the foremost centers of Buddhist studies in South Vietnam, and the La Boi Press, which established itself as one of the country's most prestigious publishing houses. He was also a founder of the School of Youth for Social Service, called "the little Peace Corps" by the American press. During the worst years of the war, he and his assistant, Sister Chan Khong, risked their lives along with thousands of other young people, including many Buddhist monks and nuns, by going into the countryside to establish schools and health clinics and to rebuild villages destroyed by the fighting. During this time he was also editor-in-chief of the official publication of the Unified Buddhist Church and the author of numerous books of poetry, Buddhist psychology, and social commentary. In 1966 he traveled to the United States to call for peace. During this trip he spoke to the American public to "describe the aspirations and the agony of the voiceless masses of the Vietnamese people." He also met with many important figures in America, including Dr. Martin Luther King Jr., who nominated him for the 1967 Nobel Peace Prize. In 1969 he led the Buddhist Peace Delegation to the Paris Peace Talks, organized to negotiate an end to the war in Vietnam. In 1973, because of his peace work, he was denied permission to return home. But being exiled did not deter him. Over the past forty years of living in the West, he has established himself as one of the most influential and respected spiritual leaders in the world. He has continued his social activism through the support of over one hundred schools and programs of village improvement in his homeland. He has also continued to be involved with peace and social justice movements around the world, speaking out on issues from AIDS to the Iraq War. With more than one hundred books in print in over thirty languages and a year-round teaching schedule, his impact continues to grow worldwide. From his hermitage at Plum Village in southwestern France, he guides numerous communities of monks, nuns, and laypersons on five continents. In 2005 he was able to return to his homeland for the first time in thirty-nine years.

In his new work, *The Art of Power,* Thich Nhat Hanh approaches the subject of power from a radically different direction than most philosophers and thinkers in the Western tradition. Beginning about 2,500 years ago in classical Greece, the topic of power and the appropriate use or abuse of power has been a central subject of debate in Western civilization. For millennia, inquiries into the subject of power have focused primarily on the state's monopoly on violence, its proper legal use, and the legitimacy and behavior of those who control it. Over the centuries, innumerable books have been written on the techniques of power, how to gain power, how to use power, and how to hold on to power.

In these pages, however, Thich Nhat Hanh begins his inquiry into power at its very base, its most organic level. He begins with volition, our deepest intention. He explains to us that the ability to attain any goal is absolutely contingent on the condition and quality of our mind. That a wholesome intention combined with a lucid mind is the prerequisite for genuine power. He reminds us of the obvious fact, so long forgotten, that anyone with a clear and caring mind is inherently powerful, no matter how little power she appears to possess. He makes crystal clear that everyone, without exception, at their core being has the deepest intention of love and goodness, and he asks, advises, exhorts, and inspires all of us to return to that primal source.

He knows all too well, having personally witnessed war and its immeasurable suffering, people's awful propensity to be corrupted by power. Like the prophet Levi, who came out of the desert to confront King Solomon, he reminds us that all power, especially great power, has within it the seeds of its own destruction. And that all the power you possess, no matter how great, is useless if it does not bring you joy and does not bring peace and happiness to those you love. He asks us how we can make the claim to be powerful when we are not free from the oppression of our anger or the scourge of our fear. He challenges us to realize that genuine power comes only with a clear mind and a calm heart, and that when we are not in control of our own thoughts we are actually quite powerless, nothing more than slaves to our fears, emotions, and craving. When this happens, it is not we who possess power; it is power that possesses us. He states boldly that every person is born with the capacity to be free of fear, delusion, and tyranny, whether external or, just as important, internal. To him both the tyranny of the state and the tyranny of our own mental anguish and its terrible effects are surmountable. He tells us that the surest way to deal with the age-old problem of the corrosive nature of state power is to create a society of insightful and healthy minds, a citizenry that is strong, happy, and free—especially free from the fear of not having power and the fear of losing power. In this book, Thich Nhat Hanh, as he begins his ninth decade, shows us the way out of the crippling paradox of corrupt power and powerlessness and points us in the direction of authentic power. He continues to walk his talk and to tell us, "I have done it, you can do it, and my friends, we can all do it." He asks us to have the courage to begin with ourselves as we express our compassion and determination to heal the world.

—Pritam Singh

THE ART OF POWER

Introduction

What does power mean to us? Why are most people willing to do almost anything to get it? Even if we are not aware of it, most of us seek to be in positions of power because we believe this will enable us to control our life situations. We believe power will get us what we most want: freedom and happiness.

Our society is founded on a very limited definition of power, namely wealth, professional success, fame, physical strength, military might, and political control. My dear friends, I suggest that there is another kind of power, a greater power: the power to be happy right in the present moment, free from addiction, fear, despair, discrimination, anger, and ignorance. This power is the birthright of every human being, whether celebrated or unknown, rich or poor, strong or weak. Let's explore this extraordinary kind of power.

All of us want to be powerful and successful. But if our drive to get and maintain power drains us and strains our relationships, we never truly enjoy our professional or material success and it's simply not worth it. Living our life deeply and with happiness, having time to care for our loved ones—this is another kind of success, another kind of power, and it is much more important. There is only one kind of success that really matters: the success of transforming ourselves, transforming our afflictions, fear, and anger. This is the kind of success, the kind of power, that will benefit us and others without causing any damage.

Wanting power, fame, and wealth is not a bad thing, but we should know that we seek these things because we want to be happy. If you are rich and powerful but unhappy, what's the point of being rich and powerful? We can use the simple, concrete, and effective practices offered in this book to cultivate real power—the freedom, security, and happiness we all want right here, right now. This is for us, our families, our communities, our society, and our planet.

The ambition to grow our understanding and compassion and to help the world is a wonderful energy that gives our lives genuine purpose. Many great teachers before us—Jesus, Buddha, Mohammed, and Moses—also had this ambition. Today we experience the same profound desire as they did: to embody peace, relieve suffering, and help people. We have seen that one person can bring liberation and healing to thousands, even millions of people. Each one of us, whether a factory worker, a politician, a waitress, a businessperson, an entertainer, or a father coaching a soccer game, shares this deep desire. But it is important to remember that to realize this wonderful ambition we must first take care of ourselves. To bring happiness to others, we must *be happiness*. And this is why we always train ourselves to first take care of our own bodies and minds. Only when we are solid can we be our best and take good care of our loved ones.

When we live without awareness, without the ability to truly see the world around us, our life is often like a runaway train. This is especially true in our professional life. If we are consumed by our jobs, we can't stop running. When we suffer in our personal lives, our professional lives also suffer. When we suffer in our professional lives, our personal lives also suffer. Heavy workloads, unrealistic deadlines, difficult working conditions, constant stress, the fear of being fired—these all cause suffering at work, which then spills into the rest of our lives. And no one, it seems, can help us. But it doesn't have to be that way. By cultivating our spiritual or true power and bringing mindfulness to our daily interactions, we can completely change the quality of our work as well as our work lives.

Mindfulness is being fully present in the here and now, being in touch with what is going on inside us and around us. Using the simple practices that follow to train our minds and focus our attention, we become not only more efficient and effective but also more relaxed and energized. *We already have enough time* to be attentive to all the people and things that are most important to us, and we can live each moment to the fullest, knowing it is a wonderful moment, the only moment we really have.

By focusing on our spiritual power, we can change our bottom line from pure profit to one that includes compassion. We don't need to get rid of profit. Compassion can bring financial and political success. I believe it is simply good business to include in our definition of the bottom line a consideration of all the effects we have on one another and on the planet. Businesses that intelligently combine profit making with integrity and concern for the world have happier employees and more satisfied customers, while making more money. Every year, *Fortune* magazine lists the one hundred best companies to work for. These companies are successful in every way. And every year, these companies share a commitment to health care, childcare, fair vacation time, respect for the environment, and profit sharing. Those admired companies understand that spending money, time, and energy caring for the physical and mental well-being of their employees and the larger community is vital to the health of their business, and more profitable.

Most politicians, and many businesses, from the pharmaceutical industry to multimedia technology development, started out with some intention of relieving people's suffering. We have to keep that intention, that ambition, alive. When financial profit overrides all other motivation, we self-destruct. The wave of corporate fraud that drowned Enron, Tyco, and WorldCom reminds us of this. That is why it is important that we conduct our professional life with compassion, with kindness. Without compassion, you can't be happy, no matter how rich you are. You become isolated and trapped within your own world, unable to relate to people or understand them.

Running after profit at the expense of compassion hurts you as much as it hurts other people.

When you look deeply, you see the pain and suffering in the world, and recognize your deep desire to relieve it. You also recognize that bringing joy to others is the greatest joy you can have, the greatest achievement. In choosing to cultivate true power, you do not have to give up your desire for the good life. Your life can be more satisfying, and you will be happy and relaxed, relieving suffering and bringing happiness to everyone.

ONE

True Power

Frederick was by conventional standards a powerful man. He was a financially successful executive who prided himself on his high ideals. Yet he was unable to really be there for himself, his wife, Claudia, or their two young sons. He was filled with an energy that always pushed him to do more, be better, and focus on the future. When his youngest son came to him, smiling, to show him a picture he had drawn, Frederick was so absorbed in his thoughts and worries about his work that he didn't really see his son as precious, a miracle of life. When he came home from work and hugged Claudia, he wasn't fully present. He tried, but he wasn't really there. Claudia and the children felt his absence.

At first, Claudia had supported Frederick and his career completely. She was proud to be his wife, and she took a lot of pleasure in organizing receptions and other social events. Like him, she was committed to the idea that getting ahead, having a bigger salary and a larger home, would increase their happiness. She listened to him to understand his difficulties. Sometimes they would stay up very late at night and talk about his concerns. They were together, but the focus of their attention and concentration wasn't themselves, their lives, their happiness, or the happiness of their children. The focus of their conversations was business, the difficulties and obstacles he encountered at work and his fear and uncertainty.

Claudia did her best to be supportive of her husband, but eventually she became exhausted and overwhelmed by his continuing stress and distraction. He didn't have time for himself, let alone for his wife and two children. He wanted to be with them, but he believed he couldn't afford to take the time. He didn't have time to breathe, to look at the moon, or to enjoy his steps. Although he was supposedly the boss, his craving to get ahead was the real boss, demanding one hundred percent of his time and attention.

Claudia was lonely. She wasn't really seen by her husband. She took care of the family and the house, did charitable work as a volunteer, and spent time with her friends. She went to graduate school and then started working as a psychotherapist. Although she found meaning in these activities, she still felt unsupported in her marriage. His sons wondered why their father was gone so much. They missed him and often asked for him.

When Frederick and Claudia's older son, Philip, had to go to the hospital for open-heart surgery, Claudia spent more than seven hours alone with Philip because Frederick couldn't get away from his business. Even when Claudia went into the hospital for her own surgery, to remove a benign tumor, Frederick didn't come.

Yet Frederick believed that he was doing the right thing by working so hard, that he was doing it for his family and for the people he worked with, who depended on him. He felt responsible for fulfilling his duties at work, and his work gave him a sense of accomplishment and satisfaction. But he was also driven by a strong feeling of pride. He was proud of being successful, of being able to make important decisions, and of having a high income.

Claudia regularly asked Frederick to slow down, to take time off for himself and his family, and to enjoy life. She told him she felt he'd become enslaved by his work. It was true. They had a beautiful home with a lush, green garden in a nice neighborhood. Frederick loved gardening, but he wasn't home enough to spend time in the yard. Frederick always responded to Claudia's requests by saying that he enjoyed his work, and his business couldn't get by without him. He often told her that in a few years, after he retired, he would have plenty of time for himself, her, and their sons.

At fifty-one, Frederick was killed instantly in a car accident. He never had a chance to retire. He thought he was irreplaceable, but it took his company only three days to fill his position.

I met Claudia at a mindfulness retreat, and she told me her husband's story. Although they lacked nothing in terms of fame, success, and wealth, they were not happy. Yet many of us believe that happiness is not possible without financial or political power. We sacrifice the present moment for the sake of the future. We are not capable of living deeply every moment of our daily lives.

We often think that if we have power, if we succeed in our business, people will listen to us, we'll have plenty of money, and we will be free to do whatever we want. But if we look deeply, we see that Frederick had no freedom, no capacity to enjoy life, no time for his loved ones. His business pulled him away. He had no time to breathe deeply, smile, look at the blue sky, and be in touch with all the wonders of life.

It is possible to be successful in your profession, to have worldly power, and be content at the same time. In the time of the Buddha, there was a very powerful and kind businessman named Anathapindika. He was a disciple of the Buddha who tried to always understand his employees, his customers, and his colleagues. Because of his generosity, his workers saved him many times from attacks by robbers. When a fire threatened to destroy his business, his staff and the neighbors risked their lives to put it out. His workers protected him because they saw him as a brother and father, and his business grew. When he went bankrupt, he didn't suffer, because his friends pitched in to help him quickly rebuild his business. He had a spiritual direction in his business life. He was inspiring and skillful, so his wife and children joined him in his spiritual practice and in caring for the poor. Anathapindika was a bodhisattva; he had a big heart and a lot of compassion.

He was happy not because of his wealth but because of his love. He allowed love to be his motivation, the force that pushed him forward. He had time for his wife and his children. He had time for his spiritual community, the sangha of nuns, monks, and laypersons practicing understanding and love. Anathapindika means "the one who helps those who are poor, destitute, and lonely." People gave him this name because he was full of loving kindness and compassion. He knew how to love and take care of himself and his family, and how to love and care for the people of his country. He always helped people when they were in difficulty, so he had many good friends.

He invested in friendship, in family, in the sangha, so he had enough time to cherish and care for the people he loved. He was very happy to serve the Buddha and his community. When people talked about the sangha, Anathapindika's eyes became bright. When people talked about poor people, his eyes became bright. When people talked about his children, his eyes also became bright.

To me what most of us call the bottom line is actually love. If we crave only power and fame, we cannot be happy like Anathapindika. Anathapindika was a businessman out of love; love was his foundation. This is why he had a lot of happiness.

Often when we start out in our profession, we do it out of love for our family, our community. In the beginning, our intentions are good. Then slowly we become consumed with pursuing success in our work. Craving for success, power, and fame replaces our focus on family and community. This is when we begin to lose our happiness. The secret to maintaining happiness is to nourish our love every day. Don't allow success or craving for money and power to replace your love. In the beginning, Frederick loved his wife, he loved his children, and he started his business with that love. But he betrayed himself by allowing his desire to succeed to take precedence over his need to love. If you look back at yourself and see that your aspiration for success is greater than your wish to love and take care of your loved ones, you know you have begun to follow Frederick.

In Buddhism, we see power differently from the way most of the world views it. Buddhists are as concerned with power as anyone else, but we are interested in the kind of power that brings happiness and not suffering.

Usually people chase financial and political power. Many people believe that if they attain these kinds of power, they can do a lot of things and make themselves happy. But if we look deeply, we see that people who are running after power suffer greatly. We suffer first in the chase, because so many people are struggling for the same thing. We believe that the power we are searching for is scarce and elusive and available only at the expense of someone else. But even if we achieve power, we never feel powerful enough. I have met people who are rich, with lots of power and fame. But they are not always happy, and some even commit suicide. So money, fame, and power can all contribute somewhat to your happiness, but if you lack love, even if you have a lot of money, fame, and power, you can't be entirely happy.

Who has more power than the president of the United States? President George W. Bush is the commander in chief of the most powerful army in the world, the leader of the strongest and richest nation in the world. Not many people have that kind of power. But this does not mean that the president is a happy person. Even with all these so-called powers, I believe he still feels powerless and suffers deeply. He is caught in a dilemma: to continue or not to continue in Iraq? Continuing with the war is difficult, and not continuing is also difficult. It's like when you eat something and it gets stuck in your throat. You cannot spit it out and you cannot swallow it. I don't think President Bush sleeps well. How can you sleep well when your young people are dying every day and every night in Iraq? How can you avoid nightmares when hundreds of thousands of people are dying because of your policy? You are very lucky you are not the president of the United States; if you were, you'd be suffering a lot right now. It is very clear that if political leaders do not have compassion and understanding as their foundation, they will misuse their power and make their own country suffer, and make other countries suffer.

Several years ago, the chief executive of one of the largest corporations in America came to the Green Mountain Dharma Center in Vermont to practice for two days with me and some monks and nuns. I was in the meditation hall leading a guided meditation one morning when I saw him sitting there. Later he talked to us about the life of a billionaire. They have a lot of suffering, worries, and doubt. They think everyone comes to them for money, to take advantage of them, and they have no friends. This man had a lot of political clout and financial resources, but he had come to learn to cultivate spiritual power. I had the opportunity to share with him some teachings on how to keep calm, breathe, and walk. He participated in sitting medi-tation, walking meditation, and eating meditation. He washed his own dishes after breakfast. I think he had a bodyguard that he did not allow to accompany him to the monastery. I gave him a small bell so that he could practice listening to the bell, coming back to his breathing, and restoring his calm in difficult mo-ments. I don't know whether he was able to continue his practice because he was utterly alone in the world of business, without a community to support him. The world he lives in is very de-manding and busy because it moves so fast.

So we have to recognize the truth that if there's no love or no deep motivation to serve this love, then no matter how rich or powerful you are, you still can't be happy. You are happy when you can relate to other people and other living beings. If not, you feel all alone, in your own world; no one understands you and you understand no one. Love is critical to our happiness.

This is true not only for individuals but also for nations. Many countries want to make progress economically, materi-ally. My definition of progress is to be happy, to be really happy. What is the use of having more money if you suffer more? You become a victim of your own success. We have to measure progress in terms of true happiness. A nation may become very rich, very developed, and be called a superpower, but the people in that country still suffer deeply. The desire for material wealth becomes more important than the health and happiness of the people. They don't have time to take care of themselves and their loved ones, and that is regrettable. To me a civilized society is one where people have the time to live their daily lives deeply, to love and take care of their family and community.

THE FIVE SPIRITUAL POWERS

What most people call power Buddhists call cravings. The five cravings are for wealth, fame, sex, fancy food, and lots of sleep. In Buddhism, we speak of the five true powers, five kinds of energy. The five powers are faith, diligence, mindfulness, concentration, and insight. The five powers are the foundation of real happiness; they are based on concrete practices we will learn in this book.

The Power of Faith

The first source of energy is faith. When you have the energy of faith in you, you are strong. In the Gospel, Jesus said that people with faith could move mountains. But the word *faith* is better translated as "confidence" and "trust," because it is about something inside you and not directed toward something external. The Zen Patriarch Lin Chi used to say to students, "You who don't have enough confidence in yourself, you go around seeking these things outside. You need to have confidence that you have the capacity to become a Buddha, the capacity of transformation and healing."

Faith is having a path that leads you to freedom, liberation, and the transformation of afflictions. If you have seen the path, if you have a path to go on, you have power. Those who have no path wander around. They suffer. They don't know where to go. You have been searching for a path, and now you have found a path; you have seen the way.

If you have some experience that this path leads in a good direction, you will have faith in your path. You are very happy that you have a path, and thus you begin to have power. This power will not destroy you or the other people around you. In fact, it gives you strength and energy that other people can feel. When you have faith, your eyes are bright and your steps are confident. This is power. You can generate this kind of power every moment of your daily life. It will bring you a lot of happiness.

If you use a method of practice and find it effective, if it brings you mindfulness, concentration, and joy, then faith and confidence are born from this, not from something other people tell you. This is faith and confidence not only in ideas but in the concrete results of your practice. When you successfully practice mindful breathing (explained in chapter 3 and Appendix A), you feel light, solid, free, and confidence is born from this kind of experience. This is not superstition. It is not relying on someone outside yourself. The energy of faith can bring you a lot of happiness. If you don't have faith, if you don't have this energy of confidence, you suffer.

If we look carefully, we can see that the energy of awakening, compassion, and understanding is already there inside us. Recognizing these energies as an inherent part of your very being, you have confidence in these energies. And if you know how to practice, you can generate these energies to protect yourself and to succeed in what you want to do.

The Power of Diligence

The second kind of power is diligence. You are capable of coming back to your best and highest self, but you must maintain this practice. Don't allow yourself to get distracted and forget to practice. Practice regularly, daily, with the support of your family, friends, and community—this is diligence. If you practice sitting meditation every day, walking meditation every day, mindful breathing every day, mindful eating every day, your practice is nourished, steadily, continuously, and this is the second source of power. You are able to practice mindfulness, but your motivation is not to prove that you are able to do it. The point is not to prove yourself. The point is to practice for your well-being and enjoyment. You simply practice, and you do it every day.

There are four aspects of diligence. The first is that when negative emotions haven't manifested in your mind, you don't give them a chance to manifest. In Buddhist psychology, we describe our consciousness as having two layers, two levels. The lower layer is called store consciousness, and the upper layer is called mind consciousness. Mind consciousness is our normal, waking mind; store consciousness is our unconscious mind.

Store consciousness is like the land, the ground, with many seeds preserved in it. In our store consciousness there are seeds of joy, forgiveness, mindfulness, concentration, insight, and equanimity. But there are also seeds of anger, hate, despair, and so on. All these seeds are kept by our store consciousness. One of the functions of store consciousness is to maintain these seeds.

When a seed is watered in our store consciousness, it manifests as an energy in our mind consciousness and becomes a mental formation. You have a seed of anger, but when the seed of anger is asleep, dormant in your store consciousness, you don't feel angry. However, when the seed is touched, when it is turned on, it becomes a mental formation called anger, and you feel the energy of anger arise. We can envision mind consciousness as a living room and store consciousness as a basement. If we water a seed of joy, that seed will manifest itself on the upper level of mind consciousness, making the living room beautiful. If we water the seed of anger or hatred, it will make the living room of our mind a hell for us and our loved ones.

We all have a seed of anger, a seed of despair, and a seed of jealousy in us. If you live in a negative environment, the environment can trigger these seeds. If you live in a positive environment, then the seeds of craving, violence, hate, and anger are not touched, not watered easily. So it is wise for you to choose a good environment that will prevent these negative seeds from being touched often. You should not allow other people around you to touch these seeds, and you should not allow yourself to water them.

When you read an article full of violence or watch a violent television program or film, you turn on the seed of violence. The first step of diligence is not to turn on these negative seeds and not to allow the environment to turn them on. Diligence here means the practice of selective watering. So if negative seeds in store consciousness haven't manifested, keep them down there, don't let them get watered. In your daily life, be careful not to give these seeds a chance to manifest. Don't suppress them; just don't give them a chance. In your community, in your family, expose yourself only to sounds and sights that will help you touch the wholesome elements within you. Try not to expose yourself to sights and sounds that stimulate the seed of craving or the seed of anger in you. You need diligence to practice this, and you may need a community or group of friends with similar values to help you create a good environment. You can encourage your partner, your children, and your friends to help you protect yourself. And you can also protect them by creating an environment where they don't have to be in touch with things that water their negative seeds.

The second aspect of diligence is calming and replacing negative seeds that do manifest in your conscious mind. When a negative seed is triggered—the seed of despair, the seed of anger, or the seed of violence—you need to know how to help it stop manifesting and return to its original form as a seed. Don't let it stay too long on the upper level of mind consciousness, because if it stays a long time, it will grow stronger and cause a lot of destruction. There are many ways to calm a negative energy without suppressing or fighting it. You recognize it, you smile to it, and you invite something nicer to come up and replace it; you read some inspiring words, you listen to a piece of beautiful music, you go somewhere in nature, or you do some walking meditation.

It's like you have put on the wrong CD, and it plays music you don't like, so you replace it with another one. When the new CD begins, it is very pleasant. The Buddha didn't have CDs in his time, so he used the image of changing a peg. A carpenter uses a wooden peg to attach two pieces of wood. When the peg is rotten, it cannot hold the two pieces together, so he removes the old one and replaces it with a new peg. In the same way, you can change your thinking if it is unpleasant. If an idea is negative, full of craving or anger, you can use mindful breathing to touch a seed that is wholesome and invite it to come up. If this wholesome seed is interesting enough, the unpleasant seed will shrivel. But the new seed should be more attractive or the unpleasant seed will not go easily and will fight for your attention. With skillfulness, with diligence, you practice the second step to change the situation, helping the negative mental formation go back to sleep and helping the positive seed manifest. When the positive mental formation arises, the living room is occupied and there is little chance for negative guests to intrude.

The first two aspects of diligence concern taking care of negative seeds, the third and fourth, nourishing positive seeds.

The third aspect of diligence is to always invite good seeds to manifest. You know that you have a seed of love, a seed of forgiveness, a seed of joy, of peace, of happiness. Learn ways to touch them and help them manifest. If you live in a good environment, where you are supported by a loving, healthy community, you have plenty of opportunities to help these positive seeds manifest.

The seeds of awakening, understanding, and compassion are always in us. They are part of our inherent nature. The question is how to help these seeds manifest. If the positive, wholesome seeds in store consciousness haven't manifested, help them manifest. Read something, say something, watch something that will water the seed of compassion, of loving kindness, so it will manifest in your mind. Organize your life in such a way that the good seeds in you can be touched several times a day, so they can manifest on the level of mind consciousness. This can be done quickly. Invite a wonderful guest to be in the living room often, and it will change the whole situation.

The fourth aspect of diligence is trying to keep a good mental formation in the living room as long as possible. We have to nourish it, to keep it in our mind. If a seed of compassion, a seed of joy, or a seed of peace is manifesting as a mental formation, it is good for you, so keep it there, invite it to stay, don't let it go back down to the basement. When you have a lovely friend visiting, you invite him to stay as long as possible, because his presence brings you a lot of joy. It is so pleasant to have a good friend sitting with you in the living room. If there is rain, you might say, "My dear friend, its raining outside, so stay and have another cup of tea." You try to persuade your good friend to stay as long as possible. The longer the mental formation stays on the level of mind consciousness, the stronger it grows at the base. This applies to the positive as well as the negative. If you entertain craving in your living room for five minutes, the seed of craving has five minutes to grow. Help the seed of craving go back to the basement as soon as possible, and invite a beneficial seed to come up instead.

When you use your skillfulness and these practices to create mindfulness, this is called true diligence. True diligence can bring a lot of joy, a lot of happiness to you and your loved ones. People with the energy of diligence are extraordinarily powerful. They can transform themselves; they can help transform the community, the environment, and the world.

The Power of Mindfulness

The third power is the power of mindfulness. Mindfulness is the energy of being aware of what is happening in the present moment. When we have the energy of mindfulness in us, we are fully present, we are fully alive, and we live deeply every moment of our daily life. Whether you are cooking, or washing, or cleaning, or sitting, or eating, it is a time for you to generate the energy of mindfulness. And the energy of mindfulness helps you know what you should do and what you should not do. It helps you avoid difficulties and mistakes; it protects you and shines light on all your daily activities.

Mindfulness is the capacity to recognize things as they are. When you are mindful, you recognize what is going on, what is happening in the here and now. When you recognize something positive, you can enjoy it; you can nourish and heal yourself just by recognizing these positive elements. And when something is negative, mindfulness helps you embrace it, soothe it, and get some relief. Mindfulness is an energy that can hold the suffering, the anger, the despair; if you know how to hold your suffering long enough, you get relief.

If we lose this power of mindfulness, we lose everything. Without mindfulness, we make and spend our money in ways that destroy us and other people. We use our fame in such a way that we destroy ourselves and others. We use our military strength to destroy ourselves and other people.

Walking and eating are actions we perform every day. But usually when we walk we are not really walking. We are being carried away by our projects and worries. We are not free. When we walk with mindfulness, dwelling in the present moment, no longer pulled by our regrets about the past or our worries concerning the future, we touch the wonders of life and each step nourishes our happiness. With mindfulness we do not have to regret the way we have lived. Mindfulness helps us see and be in touch with our loved ones. It is the energy that allows us to come back to ourselves, to be alive and truly happy.

The Power of Concentration

Mindfulness brings about the fourth power, the power of concentration. When you drink your tea, just drink your tea. Enjoy drinking your tea. Please don't drink your suffering, your despair, your projects. This is very important. Otherwise you can't nourish yourself.

There are things that you have seen but not very clearly. You can use the power of concentration to experience a breakthrough and see deeply the nature of what is there. Perhaps you have some difficulty, depression, fear, or despair, and you want to look deeply into the nature of your affliction to be able to transform it. To do this you need a lot of concentration.

Concentration can help us look deeply into the nature of reality and bring about the kind of insight that can liberate us from suffering. There are many kinds of concentration we can cultivate. Through concentration on impermanence, we become aware that everything is constantly changing. We may die tomorrow or anytime because of an accident. We should do everything we can to make our loved ones happy today. Tomorrow may be too late. With concentration on nonself—the reality that we do not have a separate self—we become aware that suffering is there not only in us but also in the other person. Not only do we suffer, but so do our children, our partners, our friends, and our colleagues. When we develop concentration on interbeing, on the interconnectedness of all things, we see that if we make them suffer they will make us suffer in return. Concentration on the nature of impermanence, nonself, and interbeing can help us realize great breakthroughs that will bring us the fifth kind of power, insight.

The Power of Insight

Insight, the fifth power, is a sword that painlessly cuts through all kinds of suffering, including fear, despair, anger, and discrimination. If you are using your powers of concentration, insight allows you to fully see what you are concentrating on.

Concentration on impermanence and nonself leads to the insight of impermanence and nonself.

Impermanence is not an idea, not a notion, but an insight. Many of us try desperately to hold on to some notion of stability or permanence. We become anxious when we hear the teaching of impermanence. But impermanence is not just negative; impermanence can be very positive. Everything is impermanent, including injustice, poverty, pollution, and global warming. In our lives, there is misunderstanding, there is violence, there is conflict, there is despair, but these things are also impermanent, and because they are impermanent they can be transformed if we have insight into how to live in the present moment.

However, sometimes we forget about impermanence. Although intellectually we realize that everything is impermanent, we forget that one day our loved ones will get sick and die. We don't remember that we ourselves have to die some day. We have a tendency to think that we will live forever. And therefore we do not have the insight we need to live beautifully and really cherish our loved ones. For many of us, the excruciating pain we feel at the death of a beloved one is not entirely because we miss him, but more because we regret that while our beloved was alive, we didn't have time for him, we didn't care wholeheartedly for him. We may have treated him unkindly. And now that our beloved is gone, we feel guilty. If we have the insight of impermanence, we know that our beloved will die one day and that we must do everything we can to

make her happy today. Don't wait for tomorrow. Tomorrow
may be too late. If we know how to live according the insight
of impermanence, we will not make many mistakes. We can be
happy right now. We can love our beloved, care for her, and
make her happy today. And we won't run toward the future,
losing our life, which is available only in the present moment.

When the Buddha spoke about impermanence, he was
speaking of insight. He was not being pessimistic but only reminding us that life is precious, that we have to treasure every
moment of life. Concentrating on impermanence in this way
will bring us the insight of impermanence. With this kind of
insight, we don't allow ourselves to be carried away by despair,
anger, or negativity, because our insight tells us exactly what to
do and what not to do to change the situation. With impermanence, everything is possible.

Without insight, we think of power as something we gain
for ourselves and ourselves alone. But another insight we can
cultivate is the insight of nonself. Nonself doesn't mean that
you don't exist; it means you are not a completely separate
entity. A lot of our suffering is born from the discrimination
between self and others and our notion of a separate self. Suppose you are a parent. Looking into your child, you will see
that your son, your daughter is your continuation. Just as a
corn plant is the continuation of a kernel of corn, the child is a
continuation of the parent. The father is there in every cell of
the son. The father and son are not exactly one person, but
they are not exactly two different people either. If the father
can see this, he touches his nature of nonself. If the son suffers,
the father suffers, and vice versa. So getting angry at your son

is getting angry at yourself. Getting angry at your father is getting angry at yourself. This is very clear. When you are able to touch your nature of no-self, when you no longer see a distinction between you and your daughter or son, your anger will vanish. When you are in a power struggle, if you know how to meditate on nonself, you will know what to do. You can stop your own suffering and the suffering of the other people in the struggle. You know that his anger is your anger, his suffering is your suffering, and his happiness is your happiness.

When my left arm hurts because of rheumatism, I try to take care of it: I massage it and do everything to bring relief to my left arm. I do not get angry at my left arm. When I have a student who suffers, who is difficult, I try to practice like this. I do not get angry at her. I try to take care of her like I take care of my own arm, because getting angry at my student is getting angry at myself and will not help the situation. But we can act with this kind of wisdom only after we achieve the insight of nonself.

In Buddhism there is a kind of wisdom called the wisdom of nondiscrimination. Nondiscrimination is one element of true love. I am right-handed, so I do most things with my right hand: brushing my teeth, inviting the bell to sound, writing calligraphy. I have written all my poems with my right hand. But my right hand is never proud of itself. It never says, "Left hand, you are good for nothing! I have to do everything by myself." And my left hand does not have an inferiority complex. It never suffers, it's wonderful. My right and left hands are always at peace with each other. They collaborate in a perfect way. This is the wisdom of no-self that is alive in us.

One day I was hammering a nail in the wall to hang a picture. I was not very skillful, and instead of hitting the nail, I hit my finger. Immediately, my right hand put down the hammer and took care of my left hand. My right hand never said, "Left hand, you know, I'm taking good care of you. You should remember that." And my left hand did not say, "Right hand, you have made me suffer. I want justice, give me that hammer!" My left hand never thinks like that. So the wisdom of nondiscrimination is there in us. And if we make use of it, there will be peace in our family, in our community.

If Hindus and Muslims in India use their wisdom of nondiscrimination, there will be peace. If Israelis and Palestinians realize their wisdom of nondiscrimination, there will be no war. If Americans and Iraqis see that they are brothers and sisters, two hands of the same body, they will not continue to kill each other. We all need to cultivate this kind of wisdom. With this insight, we can undo our own fear, suffering, separation, and loneliness, and we can help others do the same.

Insight comes from understanding. There may be elements of understanding in us already, but if we don't have time to be mindful and concentrate, insight won't manifest in us. We need to create the kind of environment where mindfulness and concentration become easy. It's like preparing the soil so that the flower we plant can sprout. Insight is the kind of understanding you obtain after you've been mindful. If you allow yourself to get lost in regrets about the past and worries about the future, it is difficult for insight to grow, and it will be more difficult to know what right action to take in the present.

It is because of ignorance that we suffer. When we begin to touch insight, we are deeply in touch with reality and there is no longer any fear. There is compassion. There is acceptance. There is tolerance. This is why we talk about insight as a kind of superpower. If you take the time to look at reality using the insights of impermanence and nonself, you will have a breakthrough that will liberate you from your suffering and your difficulties. All of the first four powers lead to this fifth superpower. And with insight comes a tremendous source of happiness.

TWO

Handling Power
Skillfully

When something upsets you, when something happens that is not to your liking in your family or your community, you want to change it right away. You are tempted to use the little power that is available to you, as a father, a mother, a teacher, *somebody*, to change the situation. This is exactly the moment to stop and contemplate. Practice looking deeply into the nature of what upsets you to see what the most mindful and compassionate response may be.

When I see one of my students not practicing mindfully, I am not happy, because I always want my students to practice well. But if this student doesn't practice well, what should I do in terms of power? I might be tempted to shout at him, to punish—to use my power and authority as a teacher aggressively. And of course a teacher always makes mistakes, especially in the first part of his career as a teacher. But to help my student, I must learn to be patient. I first need to offer him my love and insight. Using this kind of power, you are safe from misusing or overstepping your authority. You can help your student, you can help your son, your daughter, your employees without creating suffering for yourself or others.

There are many ways to share our guidance, our advice. If we share out of compassion, we will be effective and helpful. We may be unskillful in our guidance, but in the process we will learn how to share in a way that doesn't create suffering, that doesn't turn others away from us. We need to constantly check if we are guiding or teaching for the sake of fame, wealth, or a superficial kind of power.

If you cultivate the five powers mentioned in the previous chapter, you naturally begin to acquire another source of power, the power of leadership, as people turn to you for advice and influence. Three virtues are required if we are to be true leaders: the virtue of cutting off, the virtue of loving, and the virtue of insight.

The first virtue you need to use your power skillfully is *the virtue of cutting off*. Cutting off what? You cut off your anger, your craving, and your ignorance. Another way of saying this is "letting go." You gradually transform your craving, anger, fear, and delusion. If you don't have this kind of self-mastery, you can cause yourself and others great suffering, and people will not respect you. We only need to remember the many politicians and leaders whose careers were ruined by sex scandals to see the importance of cutting off the craving for meaningless sex.

This is why cutting off brings power. When you encounter someone who has the virtue of cutting off, who is free from her afflictions, you have respect for her and you listen to her. The virtue of cutting off brings liberation and lightness to body and mind. We can't buy it in the supermarket. We must attain it through our own practice.

A good leader also has *the virtue of loving*. You have the capacity to be affectionate, to accept, forgive, and embrace the other person with loving kindness and compassion. When you have this power, you are happy and people respect you—not because you shout at them or scold them, but because you offer care and compassion. People who lack compassion, love, and forgiveness suffer a lot. When you can forgive, when you can accept, you feel light, you can relate to other living beings. Without compassion, you are utterly alone. That is why compassion is the ground of happiness. If our political and business leaders can cultivate this virtue, this power of loving, they will not misuse other kinds of power: money, fame, and position in society. They will not make themselves and others unhappy.

A good leader also has to have *the virtue of insight*. Knowledge is not the same as insight. There are people with numerous PhDs, who know a vast array of scientific, philosophical, and literary discourses by heart, who can give eloquent commentaries on the Buddhist Canon, but they don't have insight, they don't have wisdom. Wisdom or insight is born from looking deeply. A genuine leader has the wisdom to show us the path out of suffering. You may be in a difficult situation, caught in confusion, and without direction. When you come to a true leader, he can show you the way. Very quickly you see a way out, because he has wisdom.

When we have insight, we can easily take care of difficulties, tension, and contradictions. If we don't have it, we just go around in circles, haunted and controlled by our suffering, fear, and worries. So the third virtue is to be able to look deeply to gain insight, so we can resolve our difficulties and help other people.

If you lead with the three virtues of cutting off, offering love, and cultivating insight, you have real authority. Simply having the title of leader is not enough. Titles do not give true power. When you practice mindfulness well and you radiate joy, stability, and peace, you acquire a much deeper authority. When you speak, people listen to you, not because they have to but because you are fresh, serene, and wise. A good leader is one who exercises only this kind of authority. She doesn't strive for it or want to use it, but it comes naturally. She inspires people by her way of living, and people listen to her because of her authenticity.

You can evaluate the quality of your authority by looking deeply to see if compassion is the foundation of your leadership. See if your authority comes to you because of your spiritual insight rather than your wealth or your position in the community. Even if you are the pope, if you don't have that spiritual life, that loving kindness and compassion, you don't have real authority. You might give orders that people follow because they are afraid of you, but this is not true authority.

If you don't practice the five powers and the three virtues of a true leader, the power you hold in your hands can turn against you, because without spiritual authority, we are always at risk of being seduced by the power we possess and abusing our power. Suppose you are an employer or a teacher. Because you are in a position of authority, you may be tempted to impose your will on your employees, your students. As a parent, you know that it can be hard not to use your power as a parent to control your children. But if you do that, you create a lot of suffering for your children and for yourself. Many people resent their parents because their parents misused their power and authority. If there is a fight between a parent and a young child, it cannot be a fair fight because the parent always has more power. Even if we have only a little bit of power, without spiritual authority, there is always a temptation to misuse it. But if we cultivate the five kinds of spiritual power, they will grow in us and we will have the capacity to transform and protect ourselves and those we love from suffering and despair.

When you have a strong desire to cultivate this power, you do everything you can to find an environment where you can be doing that all the time. I became a monk not because I wanted to be different from others or to cut myself off and live in a hermitage, but because I wanted to devote all my time to helping other people.

Imagine a president who relied on the five spiritual powers instead of political force. He would then be able to use the means available to him to bring reconciliation, peace, and happiness to people in his country as well as in other countries.

Before he left his family to become a monk, Siddhartha, the man who became the Buddha, saw that his father the king, who was politically very powerful, still felt helpless much of the time. His father saw corruption around him but wasn't able to stop it. He was still caught in fear and craving. With fear, anger, and confusion controlling us, the exercise of political power can bring only suffering to us and the people around us. One of the main reasons Siddhartha left his family and renounced the throne was his understanding that political power by itself couldn't help him or his country to be happy. Siddhartha was determined to discover another kind of power, a spiritual one.

If we look below the surface, we see that the rich and powerful still suffer a lot and create a lot of suffering around them, in spite of all their privilege. Although they have a lot of power, they often fall into the abyss of despair and suffering. Our political and economic leaders relish their power, but they also suffer because of it. It is time for us to reconsider the meaning of power and change our direction in life. The philosopher Jean-Jacques Rousseau wrote, "The strongest is never strong enough to be always the master, unless he transforms strength into right, and obedience into duty." Power will be challenged by those with less power if it is seen as illegitimate. But when power is seen as legitimate and comes with spiritual authority, it is appreciated and even revered.

When there are some who are too powerful and others who don't have any power at all, there is always a tendency to revolt. Vast inequality between people and groups makes power unstable. Even if people appear to accept those in authority, their power will always be insecure. But when power is based on spiritual authority and is a manifestation of love, wisdom, and freedom from afflictions, it can establish justice, maintain order, and withstand challenges peacefully, without resorting to violence or oppression.

Business leaders, stockbrokers, and politicians seek financial and political power. And it seems like there is never enough. Buddhists and many other spiritual seekers also want power, but they seek the powers of faith, diligence, mindfulness, concentration, and insight. These powers are unlimited, and they never do any harm to anyone, including oneself.

Many people think of money as a source of happiness. They work in part to make money. It's true that money is a kind of power. With money you can buy anything you want. Politicians promise to help you get more power and more money. People believe that a good politician can give people more buying power. Being able to buy things and choose what to buy makes people feel powerful. After all, with money you can buy not only material things but people to clean your house, care for your children, and cook your meals. You ease people's financial difficulties and then they are indebted to you; they are caught and you have more power. With your power, you can manipulate them and force them to do what you want.

With enough money, you can also buy whole nations by offering trade and special treatment. You may promise that if they take your side in a war, they will get your support in developing their economy and so on. When you have money, you have this kind of power to buy others. You have the power, but if you misuse your power you will make yourself suffer and you will make others suffer.

Money can create fame, it can buy a name, it can buy pres- tige. You can write a book and become well known even if you don't have much talent. Or you can pay someone else to write a book but take credit as the author. There are things like this going on in the world, that's how money can buy fame. When you are famous, you can make even more money. If you are a television personality, your image becomes familiar and others want you to do advertisements for their companies. You get a lot of money for just a one- or two-minute commercial. You say something good about a product, and people listen to you and buy it. Money brings fame, fame brings money, and both of them can bring other things, like sex. Because it easily corrupts us, having power can be very dangerous.

Money and fame are not evil in and of themselves. But if you don't know how to handle them, they become evil. The way you use money, the way you use your fame can lead you and many other people to suffering. If we are wise and have spiri- tual power, then money and fame will do no harm. In fact, they may be helpful. It is possible to use money and fame with wisdom to relieve suffering and create happiness. Whether money and fame are helpful or destructive depends on how we handle them.

Spiritual and political power are not mutually exclusive. Em- peror Ashoka, who reunified India in the third century B.C., ad- opted the teachings of the Buddha and became a wonderful king for all of India. He recognized in the teaching and prac- tice of the Buddha the possibility of creating a new kind of so- ciety. He limited the number of animals killed to what was necessary for all to eat. He urged people to practice compassion and understanding, refraining from killing and stealing. Emperor Ashoka had the power of a maharaja, a great king, and he used that power to help people.

In the Middle East, Israel is a superpower. Israel has sophisticated nuclear technology and a large army. Everyone knows that it has the power of striking and punishing and that it is supported by the United States. But this power is not enough to keep Israel happy and safe. That is why Israel must cultivate other kinds of power. Political leaders need to be aware of the power to be calm, the power to use loving speech, the power to understand the suffering and difficulties of other nations, the power of talking to them with love and compassion. If Israeli leaders learn how to cultivate the five spiritual powers, they will not misuse their political and military power and create more suffering within and outside the country.

If you strike out at others, they suffer, and they will strike back at you one way or another. If they cannot do it officially, they will do it unofficially. If they can't bring a bomb on an airplane, they will use bombs in other ways. Misuse of power is the primary cause of suffering for many of us. The way power is used is not just a matter of spirituality; it is a matter of life and death for a whole nation.

Business and political leaders are powerful in our society. In many ways they decide our fate. We must find ways to help them learn to use their power with wisdom. They are caught in suffering, fear, and anger, and without enough understanding and compassion, they can misuse their power. They proceed with decisions that the majority of people in their own country and around the world don't support. We shouldn't let them misuse for purposes of destruction the power we have entrusted to them. We can channel our wisdom and compassion to these political and business leaders, so a balance can be restored in them. Their spiritual power can act as a check on their political and economic power.

During the Buddha's time, there was a monk, Bhaddiya, a former governor of the Sakya kingdom. When he became a monk, he gave up everything. One day, while sitting in meditation at the foot of a tree, he said three times, "O my happiness!" Another monk overheard it and thought Bhaddiya regretted losing his power as a governor, and he reported this incident to the Buddha. The Buddha summoned Bhaddiya and asked why during the night he had pronounced "O my happiness" three times. Bhaddiya replied, "Noble teacher, when I was governor I had a lot of power, a lot of money. I had many units of soldiers guarding me. I could buy anything I wanted. But I wasn't happy because I was always fearful. I was a victim of fear, jealousy, hatred, and greed. Now I no longer have any fear or any afflictions. I don't have anything to lose. I am not afraid of being assassinated anymore. I don't need a bodyguard. I have a lot of freedom and peace. That is why I said 'O my happiness' three times. If I have disturbed the sangha, I beg for pardon."

This is a beautiful story. It shows us clearly the limitations of financial and political power, and the true power of liberating ourselves and helping others do the same.

THREE

The Art of Mindfulness

Imagine the power of our actions if each one contained one hundred percent of our attention.

Many large companies spend significant resources on research and development departments because they know that for their business to thrive, they must constantly improve and stay on top of the latest information. The same is true of figuring out how to create a mindful business: it takes an investment in developing insight that will guide you, protect you, and put you and your business on the right path.

Everything is related to everything else. Your well-being and the well-being of your family are essential elements in bringing about the well-being of your business or of any organization where you work. Finding ways to protect yourself and promote your own well-being is the most basic investment you can make. This will have an impact on your family and work environment, but first of all it will result in an improvement in the quality of your own life.

The foundation of your investment, the key to transforming your professional life, is mindfulness. Mindfulness is the energy of attention. It is the capacity in each of us to be present one hundred percent to what is happening within and around us. It is the miracle that allows us to become fully alive in each moment. It is the essential basis for healing and transforming ourselves and creating more harmony in our family, our work life, and our society. The fruit of mindfulness practice is the realization that peace and joy are available within us and around us, right here and right now. Mindfulness is one of the five spiritual powers, but it is also the foundation for acting in the world in a way that reflects our true power. Our family and professional lives will be poisoned if we don't know how to create and maintain a mindful home and a mindful workplace. Many businesses intuitively understand this truth.

Political and financial power can't fully satisfy us when we don't have mindfulness. We need the energy of mindfulness to help us come back to ourselves and look deeply into our situation. We work in a profession, but we bring to the work our own individual difficulties, pain, and suffering. Mindfulness practice allows us to embrace and understand our suffering. This is the basis for personal transformation and healing.

So how do you *do* mindfulness? It is very simple and also very challenging. The practice of mindfulness requires only that whatever you do, you do with your whole being. You have to invest one hundred percent of yourself in doing even very simple things, like picking up a pen, opening a book, or lighting a stick of incense. As a novice monk, several times a day I had to light incense to offer on the altar of the meditation hall. I was taught to pick up the stick of incense with both hands, the left hand on top of the right hand, which picks up the stick of incense. A stick of incense is very light. Why do you have to use both hands? The idea is that you have to invest one hundred percent of yourself into this simple act of picking up an incense stick. When you strike the match and light the incense, or put the tip of the incense stick into the flame of a candle, you have to be with the act of lighting one hundred percent. This is the practice of mindfulness.

When you pour tea, the act of pouring the tea into the cup can become an act of meditation if you pour with mindfulness. Don't think about the past. Don't think about the future. Don't think about what you're going to do the next day. Focus entirely on the act of pouring the tea. Invest yourself entirely in the here and now.

Everyone knows how to pour tea, everyone knows how to drink tea, but not everyone pours tea mindfully and drinks tea mindfully. This is because we have a tendency to run away from the here and now—we are driven by our habit energy. Our habit energy is strong, so we need to practice to transform it. The more we free ourselves of our habit energy, the more we will be capable of living fully every moment of our daily life.

In our work, we may be responsible for many people, a few people, or just ourselves. It's good to be responsible. We may also have the desire to be successful. But because we lack mind-fulness, we allow ourselves to be carried away by our desire for success. It becomes a habit. It pushes us all the time. We're no longer capable of drinking our tea in the here and now. Even when the tea is in our mouth, we aren't conscious of it. We're drinking our projects, we're drinking our problems.

According to the Buddha, life is available only in the here and now, the present moment. He said, "The past is already gone, the future is not yet here. There's only one moment for you to live, and that is the present moment." If you miss the present moment, you miss your appointment with life. It's so clear. Mindfulness is the energy and practice that helps you go back to the here and now so that you encounter life. It is a practice that requires time and support. Without training and without the support of a community of fellow practitioners, you won't be able to do it. There may be people you work with who are willing to become your copractitioners.

You may have a beautiful house and yard that are perfectly taken care of. There are many flowers in your yard. You know these beautiful flowers are there, but you are never able to enjoy them. When people look at your yard, they may envy you very much. They would like to have a yard like yours where they could walk and enjoy the grass, the flowers, and the trees. But you don't have time to enjoy it because you are obsessed with finding answers to questions, solving problems, overcoming difficulties, and being number one at work.

From time to time, you have a flash of insight: "I have a beautiful yard and I must make time to enjoy it." So you decide to go into the yard. You take a few steps and look at the flowers, the trees, and the grass. You have good intentions. But after four or five steps, you give up, because your preoccupation with your work is too strong. It's like a dictator. It prevents you from being present to enjoy the wonders of life that are available in the here and now.

When I was a sixteen-year-old novice monk, my teacher taught me to open the door and close the door with one hundred percent of myself. One day, my teacher asked me to get something for him. Because I loved him very much, I was eager to do it, so I rushed to do this task and closed the door quickly.

My teacher called me back: "Novice, come back here." I went back to him. I joined my palms and looked at him. He said, "Novice, this time go out mindfully and close the door behind you mindfully." That was the first lesson he gave me on the practice of mindfulness. At that moment, I began to walk mindfully and became aware of every step I took. I touched the doorknob mindfully. I opened the door mindfully. I went out and closed the door behind me mindfully. My teacher didn't have to teach me a second time how to close the door.

When you hold the hand of a child, invest one hundred percent of yourself in the act of holding her hand. When you hug your partner, do the same. Forget everything else. Be totally present, totally alive in the act of hugging. This is the opposite of the way we've been trained to lead our lives and run our businesses. We've been taught to do many things at once. We answer an e-mail while we talk on the phone; while in a meeting for one project, we work on our notes for another project. Every new technology promises to help us do more things at once. Now we can send e-mail while listening to music, talking on the phone, and taking a picture, all with the same device. With your energy that dispersed, where is your power?

Instead of always multitasking, we must teach ourselves to unitask. Mindfulness needs some training. We may be very intelligent. We may understand this right away. But that doesn't mean we can do it. To do it, we have to practice and train ourselves.

First, we use our practice of mindfulness to focus on ourselves. Once we have done this, then, with mindfulness, we look at our family. Our family, however we may identify it, is our home. We can't go straight to looking at our work life without first looking at our home base. There may be suffering, fear, or anxiety in our family. Mindfulness helps us recognize this suffering, and embrace and transform it. You can say to your loved ones, "I'm here for you. Let's embrace the pain together and transform it." Mindfulness is the capacity of being there, fully present. When you love someone, the most precious gift you can give your loved one is your true presence. You can't buy the ability to bring joy and transform suffering.

Then mindfulness will help us understand the situation at our workplace. We may be entrepreneurs—executives responsible for hundreds of people—or we may be employees, working alone or in a team. With mindfulness, we can look deeply and recognize the strengths as well as the difficulties and suffering in our organizations. When we look at our workplaces, we recognize the fears, the pain of our co-workers or employees, and we say, "I am here for you, I know you are suffering. Together we can embrace this suffering and transform it. We will do whatever we can to remove this suffering." It's the same practice we have done with ourselves and our family. With the energy of mindfulness and the capacity of looking deeply, we will find the insights to transform and heal the situation.

Mindfulness is the capacity to be present with one hundred percent of ourselves. The energy of mindfulness enables us to recognize the presence of what is. What is there is yourself, what is there is your loved ones. If you aren't capable of being in the here and now, you won't be able to recognize yourself, your happiness, or your suffering. Without your full presence, you won't be able to recognize others, and they will feel unseen, misunderstood, and unloved. They will begin to suffer, and that suffering in turn will make you suffer more. Without mindfulness, we can't help ourselves or our loved ones or succeed in our workplace. Without mindfulness, any power we have will be fleeting and ultimately unsatisfying.

Mindfulness is concrete. It can happen in a single breath. As you breathe in, keep your awareness with your breath. It may help to silently say "in" as you breathe in. And when you breathe out, silently say "out." With this simple act, your mind comes back to your body and you are truly present. It can happen in a footstep. You invest one hundred percent of your attention into taking a step. Allow your breathing to be natural, don't force it or try to change it. Be aware of how many steps you take with your in-breath, and how many you take with your out-breath. If you're practicing inside at home, you can walk very slowly, taking one step for each in-breath and one for each out-breath. If you're at work or outside, you may want to take two, three, or four steps for each in-breath and each out-breath. It may help to say "in, out" silently as you walk. For example, if you take three steps when you breathe in and four steps when you breathe out, you can say, "In, in, in. Out, out, out, out." Keep your mind completely with your steps and your breath. This practice is very easy and profoundly effective. With mindful breathing and mindful walking, you can go back to yourself and be really present and alive.

To understand mindfulness, we need to understand it on a physical level. We can learn how to go home to our bodies. We can start simply by recognizing that our bodies are there and embracing them tenderly with the energy of mindfulness. You generate mindfulness through the practice of mindful breathing and mindful walking. "My dear body, I know you are there, and I will take good care of you." Your body becomes the object of your love.

If you don't know how to take care of your body, how to release the tension in your body and give it permission to rest, you don't love your body. We all know that our bodies have the capacity of self-healing. When we cut our finger, we know that we don't have to do anything besides clean it; our body will take care of the rest. We panic when we forget that our bodies have the power of self-healing. If we simply allow our bodies to rest, our bodies can heal themselves without a lot of medicine.

When an animal in the forest gets seriously wounded, it knows exactly what to do. It looks for a secluded spot and just lies down for several days, not concerned with eating. It has wisdom. Only when the wound has healed does the animal return to foraging or hunting for food. We once had this kind of wisdom, but now we have lost our capacity to rest. We panic every time we experience something uncomfortable in our body. We rush to the doctor to get a prescription for all kinds of medicine because we don't realize that just allowing our body to rest is often the best method of healing.

There are people who complain they don't have time for a vacation. The purpose of a vacation is to have the time to rest, but even when people go on vacation they don't know how to rest. They may do lots of things and come back even more tired than before. We have to learn the art of deep relaxation. You lie down and pay attention to and relax the different parts of your body, beginning with your head and going all the way down to the soles of your feet. "Breathing in, I'm aware of my body. Breathing out, I release tensions in my body." "Breathing in, I'm aware of my eyes. Breathing out, I smile to my eyes." You continue like this with each part of your body. You scan your body, not with an X ray but with the ray of mindfulness. When you come to an organ or a part of your body that is ailing, you can stay with it longer, using the energy of mindfulness to embrace it and smile to it. This will speed the healing. You can practice this every day, alone or with your family. When you are used to it, you can lead a total relaxation session for yourself, your partner, your family. You can also encourage

others in your family to lead total relaxation for the whole
family. Children are very capable of guiding others in this
practice. When you are able to embrace your body, release accumulated tension, and help your body heal, you will be able
to go home to your feelings and emotions (this practice is explained in detail in Appendix A).

Each of us experiences pleasant feelings and painful feelings.
One of the core practices of mindfulness is to take care of our
painful emotions. Many of us run away from ourselves, from our
pain. Usually when we have pain, we don't want to face it because we don't know how to take care of it. We also think that
if we are powerful, we shouldn't feel pain. So we try to cover it
up with other things. Rather than changing the peg and helping
positive seeds arise from our store consciousness, we try to
escape our feelings through unmindful consumption. We turn
on the television, pick up a book, or talk on the phone. We try
to do something to ignore the pain, fear, sorrow, or despair we
feel. But while consuming things that help us temporarily forget
our pain, we bring more elements of distress into our bodies
and minds. We bring in the elements of craving, fear, and worries. This makes the situation worse every day.

Instead, we can go home to ourselves. We can use the
energy of mindfulness to recognize the pain inside and hold it
tenderly, like a mother holding her baby. Mindfulness is the
mother. Your pain, your sorrow, your despair, is your baby.
There is no fighting. The energy of mindfulness does the work
of recognizing, embracing, and bringing relief. When a mother
hears her baby crying, she puts aside what she's doing, goes

immediately to pick up her baby, and holds the baby tenderly. She may not know what is wrong with the baby at first, but the fact that she's holding him tenderly like this already brings relief to the baby. You may not know what is causing your pain, your despair, your depression, your fear, but if you know how to hold that pain with the energy of mindfulness, you immediately get relief, because the energy of mindfulness begins to penetrate the energy of pain, of sorrow.

Imagine a flower in the morning. The flower is not yet open. The sunshine embraces the flower, and the energy of the sunshine begins to penetrate the flower. The sun doesn't just go around the flower. The light naturally penetrates the flower, and an hour later the flower has to open itself to the sun. The sun is our mindfulness, embracing the flower of our feelings.

If we allow our anger, fear, and despair to be alone and unsupervised in us, they will be destructive. If we generate mindfulness, it will recognize and embrace these painful feelings. The practices of mindful breathing and mindful walking not only nourish and refresh us, but they also help us recognize and embrace the pain in us. Instead of using our energy, our power, to suppress our pain, we help our body become more integrated. By embracing our suffering, we are much stronger.

If our loved ones sit or walk with us, we become even stronger because the other person lends us their energy of mindfulness. We can say, "Darling, please come and do mindful walking with me. I need your presence." Then she will come and walk with you. Together, we combine our mindful energies, and there is plenty to embrace our suffering.

If we have several friends sitting with us, the positive, collective energy of mindfulness will be even stronger. It will be much easier for us to allow our pain, sorrow, and despair to be embraced by the collective energy. That is why it is so pleasant and helpful to practice in a community where everyone knows how to do the same thing. The energy is powerful. If you allow yourself to be embraced by that collective energy, you feel much better and healing happens quickly.

The energy of mindfulness helps us be aware of what is going on. When you breathe in and you know that you are breathing in, this is mindfulness of breathing. When you drink your coffee or tea and you know that you are drinking coffee or tea, this is mindfulness of drinking. When you walk and you know you are walking, and you enjoy every step you take, this is mindfulness of walking. So these kinds of practices generate the energy of mindfulness, helping you be fully alive, fully present to touch the wonders of life for your nourishment and healing.

THE FIVE MINDFULNESS TRAININGS

One time Anathapindika brought five hundred businesspeople to listen to the Buddha. The Buddha offered them a teaching that came to be known as the Sutra on the White-Clad Disciple.* It focused on how to live happily in the here and now as a

---

*During the Buddha's time, monastics wore yellow robes and laypersons wore white robes when practicing with the monastics.

businessperson and householder. In the Sutra on the White-Clad Disciple, the expression "living happily in the present moment" is repeated at least five times. Knowing that you are on the right path is the greatest happiness. The greatest happiness is having a job that you like and that expresses your understanding and compassion. Happiness, responsibility, and mindfulness are interconnected. A businessperson begins the path to happiness by taking care of himself first. With practice in generating the energy of mindfulness, he'll be able to receive the joy and happiness he deserves and he'll have the capacity to care about the well-being of others. So many elements of happiness are available right in the here and now.

This sutra taught that the foundation of mindfulness and happiness is the Five Mindfulness Trainings. These trainings are essential for learning to handle our power skillfully, for cultivating true power, spiritual power. They are the heart of mindfulness practice.

THE FIVE MINDFULNESS TRAININGS

The First Mindfulness Training

Aware of the suffering caused by the destruction of life, I am committed to cultivating compassion and learning ways to protect the lives of people, animals, plants, and minerals. I am determined not to kill, not to let others kill, and not to condone any act of killing in the world, in my thinking, and in my way of life.

The Second Mindfulness Training

Aware of the suffering caused by exploitation, social injustice, stealing, and oppression, I am committed to cultivating loving kindness and learning ways to work for the well-being of people, animals, plants, and minerals. I am committed to practicing generosity by sharing my time, energy, and material resources with those who are in real need. I am determined not to steal and not to possess anything that should belong to others. I shall respect the property of others, but I shall prevent others from profiting from human suffering or the suffering of other species on earth.

The Third Mindfulness Training

Aware of the suffering caused by sexual misconduct, I am committed to cultivating responsibility and learning ways to protect the safety and integrity of individuals, couples, families, and society. I am determined not to engage in sexual relations without love and a long-term commitment. To preserve the happiness of myself and others, I am determined to respect my commitments and the commitments of others. I shall do everything in my power to protect children from sexual abuse and to prevent couples and families from being broken by sexual misconduct.

The Fourth Mindfulness Training

Aware of the suffering caused by unmindful speech and the inability to listen to others, I am committed to cultivating loving speech and deep listening in order to bring joy and happiness to others and relieve others of their suffering. Knowing that words can create happiness or suffering, I am committed to learning to speak truthfully, with words that inspire self-confidence, joy, and hope. I am determined not to spread news I do not know to be certain and not to criticize or condemn things of which I am not sure. I shall refrain from uttering words that cause division or discord, or that can cause the family or the community to break. I shall make all efforts to reconcile and resolve all conflicts, however small.

The Fifth Mindfulness Training

Aware of the suffering caused by unmindful consumption, I am committed to cultivating good health, both physical and mental, for myself, my family, and my society, by practicing mindful eating, drinking, and consuming. I am committed to ingest only items that preserve peace, well-being, and joy in my body, in my consciousness, and in the collective body and consciousness of my family and society. I am determined not to use alcohol or any other intoxicant or to ingest foods or other items that contain toxins, such as certain TV programs, magazines, books, films, and conversations. I am aware that to damage my body or my consciousness with these poisons is to betray my ancestors, my parents, my society, and future generations. I shall work to transform violence, fear, anger, and confusion in myself and in society by practicing a diet for myself and for society. I understand that a proper diet is crucial for self-transformation and for the transformation of society.

The Five Mindfulness Trainings are a concrete expression of the practice of mindfulness and can be applied to your daily life, both professionally and in your family.* The same spirit of mindfulness exists in Christianity, Judaism, Islam, Hinduism, and all spiritual faiths. If you are from a different spiritual tradition, when you read your scriptures, when you come back to your own roots, you can identify the elements of the Five Mindfulness Trainings in your own tradition. They can help you better understand your tradition. You can't be happy if you've lost your roots.

The trainings are not imposed on us by another person; they are the direct fruit of our practice. We want to observe the mindfulness trainings because when we practice mindfulness,

*For a more extensive commentary on the Five Mindfulness Trainings, see *For a Future to Be Possible*, by Thich Nhat Hanh.

we see all the suffering that is born when we don't observe them. So we have decided to practice the five trainings to be able to uproot ill-being and suffering. They're not commandments; they're commitments made by individuals after having meditated on suffering and its causes. This is a practice. It is a determination born from our own insight. For a vivid illustration of how a highly successful company practices mindfulness and compassion based on its deep insight, see the story of Patagonia CEO Yvon Chouinard in Appendix B.

For me, the Five Mindfulness Trainings are the real practice of love, of compassion. The first training concerns the protection of life. Because I love life, because I love living beings, I'm determined to train myself in mindfulness. I am determined not to condone any act of killing in the world. Life is precious, so I am determined to protect life—not only the lives of human beings but the lives of other species, because humans are made of nonhuman elements. That means animal, plant, and mineral elements. To protect humans, we have to protect nonhuman elements. This is the teaching of the Diamond Sutra, the oldest text on deep ecology. We have to protect animals, plants, and even minerals to protect humanity. This is the essence of the first mindfulness training. If you want to protect the environment, you are invited to read the Diamond Sutra, and you will see that by protecting animals, plants, and minerals we protect men, women, and children. It is the practice of love.

The Second Mindfulness Training concerns the practice of generosity. Everywhere there is poverty. Inequality causes a lot of suffering. For this reason, we try to live in such a way as to alleviate suffering. We are determined to offer our time, energy, and material resources to those who are in need. This is real generosity. We can live more simply so that we can have more time to help others. We are determined not to steal, not to possess anything that does not belong to us. This is also the practice of true love.

The Third Mindfulness Training protects individuals and families. We make an effort to abstain from sexual misconduct and sexual abuse, because it has produced a lot of suffering. This mindfulness training is also the practice of true love. We make the commitment not to have sexual relations without love and a long-term commitment. If we look deeply, we see that the body and the mind are not two separate things. Respect for the body is at the same time respect for the mind. If there is no respect for the body, there is no respect for the mind. We cannot separate the two. Respect has to be there for love to be possible. There is no true love without respect.

In our society, we engage in a lot of empty sex, just for physical pleasure. We have confused sex with love, but this isn't love at all. When we love, we have something precious to offer: our heart, our mind. We already know that the heart and the mind are very close to our body. We have secret zones in our soul. There is pain, or there is a deep and tender aspiration that we want to keep a secret. And we share it only with the one we really love. There is a forbidden city in our soul. In the capitals of Asian countries, the king always had a forbidden city. No one outside the royal family could enter. You risked getting decapitated if you went into the forbidden city. There is a forbidden city in us that we open only to the one we love the most. It is sacred.

The same is true of our body. There is a forbidden city, areas of the body that people don't have the right to touch without our explicit permission. This wisdom is already in our culture, but to some degree we have lost our respect for the sacred zones in our body and our mind. The Third Mindfulness Training protects ourselves and others from suffering.

The Fourth Mindfulness Training is about the way we communicate. Our speech can be powerful, or we can be shouting in the wind. Never in the history of humankind have we had so many means of communication—e-mail, cell phones, faxes, television, radio, newspapers—but we still remain distant islands. There is so little real communication between the members of one family, between the individuals in society, and between nations. This is because we don't know how to listen to each other. We have little ability to hold meaningful conversation. The door of true communication has to be opened again. When we can't communicate, there's no circulation; we get sick, and as our sickness increases, we suffer and we spill our suffering on other people.

Speech can be constructive or destructive. Mindful speaking can bring real happiness; unmindful speech can destroy life. When someone tells us something that makes us healthy and happy, that is the greatest gift she can give. The Fourth Mindfulness Training also shows us that mindful speech goes together with listening deeply to others. We listen with all our attention and compassion; we are really there to receive what the other person needs to say. Our only intention is to help the other person feel safe enough to open her heart and find relief from her suffering.

The Fourth Mindfulness Training is linked to the fifth, because the Fifth Mindfulness Training is about mindful consumption—what we eat but also what we watch, read, and listen to. We are what we consume. If we look deeply into the items we consume every day, we come to know our own nature well. We have to eat, drink, and consume, but if we do it unmindfully, we may destroy our body and our consciousness, showing lack of gratitude toward our ancestors, our parents, and future generations.

We can be mindful of what we are putting into our body and consciousness. Ask yourself, "What kind of toxins am I putting into my body today? What films am I watching today? What book am I reading? What magazine am I looking at? What kind of conversations am I having?" Mindfulness is recognizing these toxins and then putting yourself on a toxin diet. You can say to yourself, "Aware of the fact that I am bringing this and that toxin into my body and consciousness every day, making myself sick and causing suffering to my beloved ones, I am determined to prescribe for myself a proper diet. I vow to ingest only items that preserve well-being, peace, and joy in my body and my consciousness."

The Five Mindfulness Trainings may seem like a big commitment that is difficult to follow. They may not fit with your image of yourself. But if you take them on, your life will be easier and your days filled with more joy. So act right away. Enter the right path and do everything you can for the protection and well-being of living beings. Then you will no longer be afraid. Even when you have to go through difficult moments, like illness, danger, or death, you'll be at peace with yourself. This has been my experience.

I know an American who enlisted in the army during the Vietnam War. He was full of goodwill and wanted to serve his country and the anticommunist cause, so he went to Vietnam, and there his duty was to murder people in the night. There were villages where the guerrillas came at night and talked to the villagers to get their support. The anticommunist government couldn't find proof that any of the villagers had collaborated with the guerrillas. But the Central Intelligence Agency said there were collaborators and they should be eliminated so the guerrillas couldn't influence the village.

The task of this American soldier was to go to the home of a suspected person at night, and with only a knife—no gun, so he wouldn't make any noise—kill this person. In the morning, the other villagers would find the person dead and say that the communists had come and killed him. In peacetime, if someone commits a crime, you bring him to court and have a trial. But in Vietnam during the war, that wasn't done. Once they believed someone was an enemy, they would just come at night and assassinate him, leaving no trace. You just eliminate the person you think belongs to the other camp. No trial, no tribunal, nothing.

Many years after the Vietnam War, the American soldier who told me this story got sick and was dying. I witnessed his suffering during that time. It was a suffering you cannot describe. It was not only suffering of the body but the utmost suffering—suffering of the spirit, of his conscience. What he had done came back to him every moment of the day and every moment of the night. It was only by fully telling his story that he was able to lay his suffering to rest.

Every act comes back to you. Your knife goes in, the person dies. Any harm you do to other people will come back and punish you. You alone will understand your suffering. No one else will understand your suffering, and the process of dying will be very difficult. This is why the greatest happiness is knowing you are on the right path. You don't do anything that destroys people, animals, plants, or minerals. With that peace of mind, you can go through difficulties and dangers without fear, and you will die in peace. This is important. There is no time to wait.

No one can practice the Five Mindfulness Trainings perfectly, not even the Buddha. The goal is not to be perfect but simply to be mindful of ourselves, even when we make mistakes. If you are lost in a forest at night, you can follow the North Star to find your way out. You follow the North Star, but your goal is to get back home; it's not to arrive at the North Star. The mindfulness trainings are like the North Star; we don't have to be perfect in practicing them. They are our guide, and we know we're on a good path. If you have a spiritual path, the path of love, compassion, and understanding, you feel happy because you know where you're going. You are on the path of compassion, of protecting life so that happiness becomes possible. That is very important. You are protected by the practice of the Five Mindfulness Trainings.

The Five Mindfulness Trainings have a universal nature. Practicing them, you become a better friend of the Buddha, a better disciple of Jesus. The Buddha, Jesus, Abraham, and Mohammed are our companions on the way. The Five Mindfulness Trainings are a practice that protects and supports us.

FOUR

Getting What We Really Want

With the practice of mindfulness and the mindfulness trainings, the motivation behind our desire for power becomes
clear. When we are clear about our motivations, our actions are
much more powerful because we can do them with one hundred percent of our intention.

Volition is the driving motivation behind our thinking,
speech, and actions. It determines everything. Every one of us
has a strong goal for our life. We want to achieve something.
We feel a ball of energy in us, a tremendous, powerful source
of energy. We want to feel truly alive.

We search for this feeling in different ways. There are
people who are ready to die for a cause. They want national
independence, they want social justice, they want to overthrow
a dictatorial regime, and they're ready to sacrifice their lives for

it. Their desire gives them the energy and strength needed for their activities. There are people motivated by the desire to protect the environment. They're willing to undergo any kind of hardship to protect the earth. There are those who want to get off the spiral of escalating consumption. They want to live a simple life to have more time and energy to serve living beings.

There are also people whose motivating desire is not so wholesome. They live only to accumulate wealth, influence, and recognition. They want to be admired and envied by others, drive fancy cars, have famous and attractive lovers, and live in luxurious houses. Then there are people whose strongest desire is to punish those they believe have caused them a lot of suffering. They live only for revenge. They focus their whole lives around the desire to attack, destroy, punish, and cause suffering to the people they think made them suffer. They're ready to blow up an airplane or force their way into an embassy carrying a bomb, losing their own lives in the explosion, just because they want revenge. They consider themselves victims of injustice, and they want to inflict sorrow and pain on other groups or other nations. This kind of motivation is the foundation of their lives and the basis of their actions. These people have given up on happiness, because if your motivation is to punish someone else or to run after fame, glory, and power, you are going to suffer a lot.

To illustrate the tragic power of our volition, the Buddha used the example of a young man who's being dragged toward a pit of fire by two strong men. The man wants to live; he's being dragged against his will. But the two men are stronger than he is, and they intend to throw him into the pit of fire. He doesn't want to die, but he can't resist. The Buddha asked, "Who are these two strong men who try to bring you to the realm of hell? They are your volition, your desire to run after what you believe to be happiness, namely the objects of your craving: craving for fame, craving for power, craving for sex, craving for wealth."

Before Siddhartha became the historical Buddha, he undertook six years of practice to become a free person, enlightened and emancipated. He had witnessed much suffering in his family, his society, and his country. He left his family and his position as a prince in his father's kingdom, but he was motivated by love, not by a desire to run away from his responsibilities. Siddhartha wanted to uproot the suffering in himself in order to offer others a way out. This was his deepest desire, and it brought him tremendous happiness. It gave him the courage and strength to go through many hardships.

We call this desire, this volition, *bodhicitta*. Bodhicitta is the mind of love, the mind of enlightenment. It can also be translated as the "mind of understanding," because understanding is the foundation of love. If you don't understand, it is not possible for you to accept and to love. If you don't understand your father, you cannot really love him. If you don't understand your daughter, you cannot love her. Understanding is love and love is understanding. And if you have the desire to attain this understanding, you have the beginner's mind, the most powerful kind of energy there is. With this energy you will never give up, because you are seeking happiness, for yourself and for others.

So all of us must look deeply into our desire. What's our true motivation? We know that business is for making money, but we have to understand what goes along with the profit we're making. Are we causing suffering, despair, or injustice in the process of making a profit? Earning money is just one part of the picture. The way we use money is also important. Money can be used to promote well-being. With money we can buy medicine and save someone's life. With money we can provide food for people who are hungry. But with money we can also destroy our own lives and the lives of others. We have to look deeply to see whether money is the only element that can bring happiness.

What's the motivating desire of people working in business, politics, the entertainment industry, sports, or science? Is it more power, more fame, more wealth? We may think that these things are only means for us to be more effective. But they will not, by themselves, help us be happy or help others. We may be misguided by our sense of pride and responsibility. We may be fooling ourselves. It's important to look deeply into our deepest desire to see its true nature. If you suffer and make your loved ones suffer, there is nothing that can justify your desire.

You may never have had a chance to practice looking into your intentions, but if you do, you will discover your deepest motivations. We have to identify the source that motivates our actions every day. A wholesome motivation will bring us well-being, it can bring happiness to us and many other people. An unwholesome motivation will bring suffering to us, our family, and many people in society.

We can distinguish our compassionate ideals from our unwholesome desires and cravings. These two things are very different, but sometimes we mistake our craving and desire for noble ideals. We often try to fool ourselves to feel more peaceful. Greed is based on ignorance. We have misperceptions. We think that if we can obtain certain things, we'll be happy. But when we get them, we continue to crave and suffer.

The Buddha used the image of the bait and hook to illustrate this. You see the bait and you think it will give you a lot of pleasure, a lot of happiness. But when you bite it, the hook gets you. These days people use lures, artificial bait, when they go fishing. The bait is not a real insect anymore but is made of plastic. It's very appealing. When the fish sees the bait, he bites the lure, because he doesn't know there's a hook inside. When the fish bites, he gets hooked and is pulled out of the water.

We're just like the fish that gets hooked. What's appealing to you? You're tempted, you want it, so you bite it, even though you know that *it* will get *you*. Fame, sex, power, and wealth are the four kinds of bait that have a hook. If you're motivated by any of these desires, your destiny is suffering. When you're wealthy, you feel powerful and important. There are so many favorable conditions encouraging you to indulge in this kind of consumption. But you can destroy yourself, your family, and even your company, and this destruction often contributes to damaging the environment and society in general.

Is our strong desire to serve our loved ones, to serve ourselves, other living beings, and our planet, or is it to strive after
lures that are empty of real nourishment? We may deceive ourselves into thinking that our concern with wealth, power, and
fame is really only a means for us to be more effective in bringing happiness to others, providing jobs, or helping the environment. But we may be misguided by our pride and sense
of responsibility. We shouldn't fool ourselves. We have to be
really honest and practice deeply to discover the true nature of
our desire and motivation. It's important to distinguish between
the indulgence of craving and true happiness. Happiness exists
in many forms, but true happiness doesn't come from the four
objects of craving: sex, power, fame, and wealth.

The Buddha described a dog who, when thrown a bare
bone, runs after it and chews on it even though there's no meat
on the bone. He doesn't get any nutrition from the bone, yet
he hangs on to it and won't let go. Our attitude is just like that.
Cravings can never bring satisfaction, yet we keep on running
after them.

The Buddha also cited the example of holding a torch
against the wind: the torch will burn your fingers. Sensual
desire is like that—it burns you. It doesn't give you true happiness; it burns you and in fact can destroy you.

The Buddha gave another example. You're thirsty and you
go into an apparently empty house. You see a bottle of water.
You're very thirsty and you want a drink. But just as you bring
the bottle to your lips, someone appears and says, "Don't drink
this water, it has poison in it." But since you're so thirsty, you

drink it anyway. Our desire for the four cravings can be like that.

Sometimes your intellect tells you that it's dangerous to embrace this or that object of desire. You know that you'll suffer, but you can't resist and you do it anyway. Without a wise friend, without a spiritual community that can protect and help you, you often do such things in spite of your better judgment.

We crave something because we don't see the true nature of the object of our craving. Don't despise money, sex, power, and fame: just look deeply to see how running after things like these has brought you a lot of suffering and little satisfaction. These cravings are like saltwater: the more you drink, the thirstier you become. We keep running after money, believing that when (and only when) we have a certain amount of money, we will be happy. Then that day comes and we have that amount of money, but it's not enough because we always want to have more.

Indulging our cravings can kill us. The Buddha used a final example of a small bird that has stolen a piece of meat from a butcher. The bird flies up in the sky, and suddenly a bigger bird comes along and tries to take the piece of meat. The little bird doesn't let go. If the little bird doesn't release the piece of meat, the big bird will kill her to get the piece of meat. The little bird knows this on some level, but she still cannot bring herself to let it go.

In fact the thing we are running after is just a delusion, and with mindfulness, we can see that it is not worth it. We can explore deeply the nature of that object of craving—let's say it's money—and then we will see that money is not something we need to crave. We need some for basic use, but not much. When you see deeply the true nature of the object of your craving, you will be healed from your running and able to finally feel free.

Deep in every one of us there is a desire to be continued, a desire for procreation. Monks and nuns also have this desire to procreate, to be continued. But it is possible for them to fulfill this desire spiritually. They can have spiritual children and grandchildren. They can completely satisfy their desires without suppressing themselves. Fulfillment through sublimation is possible with practice.

Love in a couple relationship has to do with this desire to be continued. This doesn't mean that procreation is the only valid reason for a sexual relationship. When you love, you need to express yourself. Sexual expression is one way you demonstrate your love. But I would like to tell you that it is not the only way. If you think it is the only way, you are wrong. There are many ways of expressing our love other than sexually. We can still be happy together. If you don't see things clearly and you think sex is the only way to express your love, you can become obsessed with sex. When a mother holds her child, there's a lot of love in her. When a father speaks to his son on the telephone, he can express his love deeply.

The question is how to express your love and preserve happiness. If you don't respect the other person's body, this is not love. If the sexual act does not include respect, gentleness, compassion, and loving kindness, I wouldn't say it is a true expression of love. It is an expression of craving, violence, and disrespect. So it should be made clear that in sexual expression, true love should exist; otherwise you are creating suffering for yourself and the other person. A genuine expression of love should include the desire to offer happiness, remove suffering, and remove separation. This is why sex can be deeply spiritual. It can be a very beautiful act.

When the element of disrespect is there, love is destroyed. You have to ask yourself whether the sexual act is creating suffering or not. Sometimes your partner is not in the mood to make love. If you force him, there is no respect, no love. It's like inviting someone for tea. If the person is so busy, doesn't have the time, or doesn't like tea, and you force her to sit down and have tea with you, you are not a true friend; you are not being truly loving. Respect is the first ingredient of true love. Not only for mind and spirit, but for the body. You treat her body gently and with a lot of respect, because we are made of body and mind together. In Plum Village, every time we offer massage to a person, we join our palms and breathe first. We should have complete respect before we touch the other person's body. If you are motivated by craving, sex can be destructive. If you create jealousy, anger, or frustration, you know it is not true love. So it is possible for us to express our love through sexual intimacy, but we should remember that it must be a real expression of true love, not craving. And second, we should remember that sexual expression is not the only way to express our love.

We know it's dangerous to run after objects of craving. Happiness is possible, but not through indulging desire and sensual pleasure. Real happiness is found in the knowledge that ignorance is the ground of all desire. If you know exactly what the danger is and what suffering it will bring, then that desire will die down. You know that if you get AIDS, you will suffer and you may well die. If you understand that clearly, you'll be very careful to protect yourself from contracting AIDS. Thus understanding is the foundation of correct behavior, and ignorance is its opposite.

Right or wrong action can be determined by using the single criterion of suffering or nonsuffering. Whatever causes suffering in the present or the future, for ourselves and people around us, is the wrong thing to do. What brings well-being in the present and the future is the right thing. The criterion is clear.

To put it another way, what comes from mindfulness, concentration, and insight is right, and what goes against mindfulness, concentration, and insight is wrong. Suffering and happiness are a complementary pair we can use to see our situation more clearly. If you use these two yardsticks, you'll know what's wrong and what's right, what is to be done and what shouldn't be done.

This is why, to be happy, to be a real bodhisattva, we need to take some time each day to sit down, look into ourselves, and identify the kind of energy that's motivating us and where it is pushing us. Are we being pushed in the direction of suffering and despair? If so, we must release this intention and find a more wholesome source of energy. Our volition should be bodhicitta, the mind of love, the intention to love and serve.

There are seeds of awakening and compassion in each of us. In Buddhism, a bodhisattva is someone who is awake, mindful, and motivated by a desire to help others wake up, be mindful, and be happy. Your purpose is to wake up to the reality of suffering and its causes, to wake up to the possibility of happiness. The path of understanding and compassion is the path to happiness.

If you don't have this strong desire to help people, to liberate, to bring awakening and joy, you can't be called a bodhisattva and you don't have a path to follow. But with mindfulness and awareness of our intention, we can all quickly and easily become bodhisattvas, awakened beings committed to the protection of all beings. If you have in you a lot of compassion and a lot of insight and awakening, you can act as a bodhisattva in the form of a businessperson, an athlete, a scientist, a politician, an entertainer, or a parent. The bodhisattva practices the art of living happily in the here and now and shows up in many guises. You don't have to wear a monk's robe. You don't have to have achieved enlightenment or have a certain income. You don't have to have achieved anything. You can wear a suit and tie or a pair of jeans and still carry a bodhisattva's joy, happiness, and freedom. And when you have a lot of joy, happiness, and freedom, you can share it with other living beings.

A bodhisattva may have blocks of fear, suffering, and pain within her, so she returns to herself to recognize the blocks of suffering and fear, embrace them, and transform them into compassion, love, understanding, and solidity. The bodhisattva has the ability to go back to himself to take care of his body and consciousness. Pain is an inevitable part of life, but happiness is possible. This is the summation of the Buddha's Four Noble Truths. These truths are equally applicable to businesspeople, monastics, and everyone in between. The First Noble Truth is that suffering exists. The Second Noble Truth is that suffering has causes. The Third Noble Truth is that happiness is possible. The Fourth Noble Truth is that there is a path that leads to happiness. We have to distinguish between the first truth and the third one. The first is called *dukkha* in Sanskrit, suffering. The third is called *sukha*, happiness. They are quite different. Very often, we mistake our desire or craving for happiness.

We don't need to be afraid of suffering; we can confront it. If you try to run away from it, you will never have a chance to transform it. The Buddha taught that we should look at suffering in terms of nutriments. You have consumed in a way that has brought about suffering. He said, "What has come to be— namely ill-being—if you can look deeply into its nature and identify its source of nutriments, you are already on the path of emancipation."

All of us who want to be bodhisattvas will have to do the same. We have to go back to ourselves, take good care of ourselves, and recognize the suffering in ourselves in order to embrace and transform it. You have to make time for yourself and be there for yourself. Then you will be able to be there for your family and your company, your constituents, your school, and your community.

If you are an artist or a teacher, a parent or a politician, you have the ability to be a bodhisattva and awaken many people at once. When you are motivated by this big desire, you have so much joy and energy that fame and power no longer attract you. You become active, day and night, helping people touch their seeds of joy, peace, and happiness, helping them understand and transform their seeds of discrimination, fear, and craving. Fame, political power, and financial success can't be compared with the joy of knowing that your life on earth is beautiful and helpful. You are a bodhisattva manifesting in the here and now.

Whatever your business, if your true intention is to be a bodhisattva at your work, then you are being a buddha, even if you do not call yourself one. This is what Anathapindika did as a bodhisattva businessman.* This is something anyone in any profession can do: be truly present, fully alive with a compassionate heart. With the support of a community, this practice can bring transformation, healing, joy, and happiness. You and your family become one entity. You are participating in the work of promoting awakening and transformation. It's a wonderful path.

Power is good for one thing only: to increase our happiness and the happiness of others. Being peaceful and happy is the most important thing in our lives and yet most of the time we suffer, we run after our cravings, and we look to the past or the future for our happiness.

---

*Anathapindika was a good friend of the Buddha first mentioned in chapter 1.

We know that the bottom line of business is profit. But *to profit* means "to benefit from." There are many ways one can benefit from being a bodhisattva. If our work brings about well-being, there's nothing wrong with making money. It's possible to make money in a way that is not destructive, that promotes more social justice and more understanding and lessens the suffering that exists all around us. To do this, we need to be free from the pursuit of power, wealth, fame, and sex. These four go together. If you don't practice mindfulness, you'll be the victim of these four lures. Looking deeply, we see that it's possible to work in the corporate world in a way that brings a lot of happiness, both to other people and to us. When we're doing something for the benefit of all humankind and the environment, our work has meaning. Even if it's also making money, it has meaning, because it can bring well-being to the world.

FIVE

The Secret of Happiness

If we are able to quiet the cravings within us, we see that our true desire is not wealth or fame but happiness. Because we want happiness, we search for power outside of ourselves. But as long as we seek power and happiness in fame, money, and sex, we will not find it. Only by coming back to ourselves and purifying our minds can we experience true, lasting happiness and the kind of power that can't be corrupted.

Is it possible for those of us who are poor, who are unknown, to have happiness? Many of us think that if we have no money and no fame, we have no power and therefore cannot be truly happy. Of course, our basic material needs for food, water, shelter, clothing, physical safety, and livelihood must be met for us to be happy. Abject poverty leads to suffering, disease, and violence. So I am speaking here of the desire to have money above and beyond our material needs.

When the Buddha attained enlightenment, he wasn't famous. On that remarkable day he was unknown to most of the world. Even his family did not know that he had become enlightened. When he went to Deer Park to see the five friends with whom he had previously practiced, they did not know he had attained buddhahood. He wasn't famous yet. After he attained enlightenment, he sat down at the foot of the bodhi tree and played with children and was very happy. His happiness was not based on fame or money. His happiness was based on his liberation, his peace, and his wisdom. We should train ourselves to see happiness in terms of peace, freedom, and compassion, not the size of our bank accounts. These are tremendous sources of power that we can cultivate in our daily lives. Later in his life the Buddha did become famous. But this fame couldn't consume and destroy him; this fame only helped his teaching and practice to spread farther. This kind of fame was not evil; in fact, it was of great benefit to many living beings.

Even if you have no money or fame, the practice of the five powers can make you happier than a lot of people with great wealth and celebrity. Surprisingly, when you are happy, it is not difficult to earn enough money to live comfortably and simply. It is much easier to make the money you need when you are solid and free. If you are happy, you are more likely to be comfortable in any situation. You are not afraid of anything. If you have the five spiritual powers and you lose your job, you don't suffer much. You know how to live simply, and you can continue to be happy. You know that sooner or later you will get another job, and you are open to all possibilities.

We must distinguish happiness from excitement, or even joy. Many people think of excitement as happiness. They are thinking of something, or expecting something that they consider to be happiness, and for them, that is already happiness. But when you are excited you are not peaceful. True happiness is based on peace.

Suppose you are walking in a desert and you are dying of thirst. Suddenly you see an oasis and you know that once you get there, there will be a stream of water you can drink from so you will survive. Although you haven't actually seen or drunk the water, you feel something—excitement, hope, joy, but not happiness yet. Happiness comes only once you actually drink the water and your thirst is quenched. If you don't have peace in yourself, you haven't experienced true happiness.

Some people find it easy to be happy and others don't, even though they have plenty of conditions for happiness. You can buy conditions for happiness, but you can't buy happiness. It's like playing tennis. You can't buy the joy of playing tennis at a store. You can buy the ball and the racket, but you can't buy the joy of playing. To experience the joy of tennis, you have to learn, to train yourself to play. It's the same with writing calligraphy. You can buy the ink, the rice paper, the brush, but if you don't cultivate the art of calligraphy, you can't do calligraphy. So calligraphy requires practice, and you have to train yourself. You are happy as a calligrapher only when you have the capacity to do calligraphy. Happiness is also like that. You have to cultivate happiness; you cannot buy it at the store.

Walking meditation is a wonderful way to train yourself to be happy. While standing in one spot, look off a little ways and choose something—say, a pine tree. Make up your mind that while walking to the pine tree you will enjoy every step, that every step will provide you with the kind of peace and happiness that nourishes, heals, and satisfies.

There are those of us who are capable of walking from one point to another in that way, enjoying every step we take. We are not disturbed by anything—not by the past, not by the future, not by projects, not by excitement. Not even by joy, because in joy there is still more excitement than peace. If you are trained in walking meditation, with each step you can experience peace, happiness, and fulfillment. You are capable of truly touching the earth with each step. You see that being alive, being established fully in the present moment and taking one step, can be a wonder, and you live that wonder in every moment of walking.

Whether we are walking alone or together as a community, every step releases tension so we can touch the wonders of life right here and now. When you are free from tension, free from regrets about the past and worries about the future, you can touch the Kingdom of God or the Pure Land of the Buddha with every step you take, all day long. In the Gospel, there's a story of a farmer who discovered a treasure in a field. He went home and sold everything to buy that field. Like that farmer, if we know how to touch the Kingdom of God or the Pure Land of the Buddha in the here and now, we have the most precious treasure already and we don't need to run after money, fame, and power anymore. I have been urging church leaders and spiritual leaders to provide us with the kind of teaching and practice that will help us touch the Kingdom of God right here, right now, so we won't run after fame, sex, money, and power anymore. The Kingdom of God is always available. The question is whether we are available to the kingdom. In Buddhist teachings, it is said that the Pure Land of the Buddha is in your heart. If you are free, you can touch the wonders of life here and now. The French writer André Gide said that God is happiness. I like that. He also said that God is available twenty-four hours a day. If God is there, his kingdom is there. But are you there to enjoy the kingdom? The same thing is true in Buddhism. If you do walking meditation properly, every step helps you touch the Pure Land of the Buddha. So you can challenge yourself: "I will do walking meditation from here to that pine tree. I vow that I will succeed." Only if you are free can your steps bring you happiness and peace.

One nun shared with me a story about her friend who visited Plum Village. Her friend is married and has a family, a job, a house, a car, and everything she needs. She thinks of her relationship as a good one, although it wasn't what she'd expected. Her job is enjoyable, with a salary above average. Her house is beautiful.

And yet she doesn't feel happy. Intellectually, she knows that in terms of comfort she has everything, but it does not keep her from being depressed. Not many people are as successful as she is, and she knows that she is fortunate. And yet she isn't happy.

We have a tendency to think of happiness as something we will obtain in the future. Like the oasis visible from miles away in the desert, we expect happiness down the road. We don't have certain conditions we think we need to be happy, but we believe that once we have them happiness will be there.

Suppose you think a degree will make you happy. You think about the diploma day and night, and you do everything to get it because you believe that happiness will be there tomorrow, when you earn your diploma. There may be joy and satisfaction in the days and weeks after you receive your diploma, but you will quickly adapt to that new condition, and in just a few weeks you won't feel happy anymore. You will get used to having a diploma. We become immune to our happiness, and after a while we don't feel happy any longer.

Even people who win the lottery and become millionaires don't often get lasting happiness from their good fortune. Studies have found that after two or three months winners return to the emotional state they were in before winning the lottery. During those three months, what they experience is not exactly happiness; there is a lot of thinking, a lot of excitement, a lot of planning. But three months later, they fall back to exactly the same emotional level they were in before winning the lottery.

Perhaps you want to marry someone, thinking that if you can't marry her, then you cannot be happy. You believe that your happiness will be great after you marry that person. After you marry, you may have a period of happiness, but eventually happiness vanishes. There is no longer any excitement, any joy, and of course no happiness. What you get is not what you expected and dreamed of. Perhaps you know that what you have attained will not last. The person you are living with may betray you one day. You can't be sure that person will be faithful to you, so there is also fear and uncertainty. Even if you have a good job, you are not sure you can keep it: you may be laid off at any time. This type of happiness without peace has an element of fear and cannot be true happiness. To hold on to these conditions of so-called happiness, you have to be busy all day long. And with these worries, uncertainties, and busyness, you don't feel happy and you become depressed.

Even after we obtain all the conditions we believe are necessary for our happiness, we remain unsatisfied. So the question for those of us who want true happiness is, what can we rely on? The answer is simple and profound. Those of us who want to experience great happiness, to awaken the mind of great understanding and love, should not base our mind on any external thing, including form, sound, touch, and ideas. We should not rely on any object to give rise to the mind of enlightenment, the mind of love.

Suppose you wonder what path to choose for your life. You may think that being a police officer will make you very happy. Some people may be attracted to this path because they want the uniform, they want power. Others feel they can find happiness as medical doctors. And there are those who feel they can be happy only if they become politicians.

You must choose one of these paths, but you are not sure it will bring you happiness. You hesitate, wondering, "If I am not

happy in this career, what will I do?" We have this doubt because we are basing our decision on form, on appearance. The
path of a monastic is a form. The path of a politician is a form,
just like the path of a businessperson and the path of an
artist. There are artists who are happy and artists who aren't.
There are monastics who are happy and monastics who
aren't. There are laypersons who are happy and laypersons
who aren't. There are police officers who are happy and police
officers who aren't. So you cannot say that the position or oc-
cupation you long for will make you happy. If you think you
can base your decision and your happiness on this kind of
outer form, you are wrong. You will be deceived.

You may want to marry a man who is attractive, who has
a prestigious degree, or who has a high position in society,
because you think that marrying such a person will guarantee
your happiness. If you want to marry someone just because
he is beautiful or rich, you are relying on only the external
form, and this changes constantly. What if your spouse loses
his job, his fame, his power? What if he gets into an accident
and is no longer attractive?

Whatever form you take, whatever path you take, if you are
attached to the form, you cannot get the happiness you want,
even if you become a monk or a nun. If you are attached to the
form of a monastic and you think that wearing the robe and
living in the monastery will make you happy, you are wrong.
There are monks and nuns who are not happy because they are
not capable of being understanding and loving. But when you
know how to cultivate understanding and compassion in every

moment of your life, the outer form of your life doesn't matter anymore. So the key to success is not the form of a monastic or layperson, of a police officer, a farmer, or a doctor, but your capacity to cultivate happiness, understanding, and compassion.

Wherever there is form, wherever there is perception, there is delusion. We have to be very careful about basing our decisions on the appearance of things, on the outer form. To find happiness, enlightenment, and compassion, you have to be free, not fooled by your perceptions. When you look at something deeply, you discover its nature and you are no longer fooled by it. Since you are not fooled by the appearance, you no longer suffer, and you have the capacity to be happy.

We tend to think, "I'll be so happy if I can get this and this and this. But if I'm not able to get these things, my life will be ruined, and I'll never be happy." Our ideas about what power is and what will bring us happiness can be quite dangerous for us. It's dangerous to be committed to an idea of happiness, because then you're caught in that idea. Happiness can come to you in a thousand ways if you only allow it to. But if you're committed to only one idea of happiness, you're stuck. Happiness can no longer come to you because you've decided that you'll refuse everything except this one path of happiness. Of course you're motivated by the desire to be happy and to make the people you love happy. But the idea of happiness that you have may actually be an obstacle preventing you and your beloved ones from being happy.

The Buddha told the story of a merchant, a widower, who went away on a business trip and left his little boy at home.

While he was away, bandits came and burned down the whole village. When the merchant returned, he didn't find his house; it was just a heap of ash. There was the charred body of a child close by. He threw himself on the ground and cried and cried. He beat his chest and pulled his hair.

The next day, he had the little body cremated. Because his beloved son was his only reason for existence, he sewed a beautiful little velvet bag and put the ashes inside. Wherever he went, he took that bag of ashes with him. Eating, sleeping, working, he always carried it with him. In fact, his son had been kidnapped by the bandits; three months later, the boy escaped and returned home. When he arrived, it was two o'clock in the morning. He knocked on the door of the new house his father had built. The poor father was lying on his bed crying, holding the bag of ashes, and he asked, "Who is there?" "It's me, Daddy, your son." The father answered, "That's not possible. My son is dead. I've cremated his body and I carry his ashes with me. You must be some naughty boy who's trying to fool me. Go away, don't disturb me!" He refused to open the door, and there was no way for the little boy to come in. The boy had to go away, and the father lost his son forever.

After telling this story, the Buddha said, "If at some point in your life you adopt an idea or a perception as the absolute truth, you close the door of your mind. This is the end of seeking the truth. And not only do you no longer seek the truth, but even if the truth comes in person and knocks on your door, you refuse to open it. Attachment to views, attachment to ideas, attachment to perceptions are the biggest obstacle to the truth."

It's like when you climb a ladder. When you get to the fourth rung, you may think you are on the highest step and cannot go higher, so you hold on to the fourth rung. But in fact there is a fifth rung; if you want to get to it, you have to be willing to abandon the fourth rung. Ideas and perceptions should be abandoned all the time, to make room for better ideas and truer perceptions. This is why we must always ask ourselves, "Am I sure?"

I have a friend who became a stockbroker. At first, he was quite eloquent and used that talent to persuade his clients to buy stock. But after encountering the Buddhist teaching and learning the mantra "Are you sure?" he changed his views and his method. When people asked him whether he was sure, he said, "I can't say that I'm sure. This is my opinion, based on my best understanding at this time." He was honest. The result was that even more people sought his advice.

We may find that ambition—the desire to become someone special—is very strong in us. Achieving and "becoming someone" is seen as significant, yet it can lead us to suffer a lot in spite of our many achievements. How can we deal with the desire to become someone?

Your action, what you do, depends on who you are. The quality of your action depends on the quality of your being. Suppose you want to offer happiness to someone. You are eager to make a person happy. This is a good idea, but if you yourself are not happy, you can't do it. To make another person happy you have to be happy yourself. So there is a link between doing and being. If you don't succeed in being, you can't succeed in doing.

Happiness becomes possible when we realize we have a path, when we know where we are going. If you don't have the impression that you are on the right path, if you don't know where you are going, you suffer, you feel lost and confused. Happiness is feeling that you are on the right path every moment. You don't need to arrive at the end of the path to be happy. You are happy right here and right now.

Being on the "right path" has to do with the very concrete ways in which you live your life in every moment. It is possible to live mindfully every moment of your daily life. This makes you happy, and it also makes the people around you happy. Even if you haven't "done" anything yet to make them happy, once you are walking that path and you are happy doing so, you become pleasant to be with, fresh, and compassionate, and people benefit from being around you. Look at the tree in the front yard: the tree doesn't seem to do anything. It just stands there, vigorous, fresh, and beautiful, and everyone benefits from it. That is the miracle of being. If a tree is less than a tree, all of us will be in trouble. If a tree can be a real tree, there is hope, there's joy.

So if you can be yourself, this is already love, this is already action. Action is based on nonaction, and nonaction is the practice of *being*. There are people who "do" a lot, who cause a lot of trouble. Even if they have the best of intentions, the more they try to help, the more trouble they create. There are a lot of activists around us who are not peaceful, not happy, and so what they do causes more trouble. This is why what we want to do is to *be* in such a way that peace and compassion are possible in every moment. Words and actions coming from that foundation can be only helpful. If you can make a person suffer less, make her smile, you will feel very happy, very rewarded.

If a nun is happy, it is not because she has power or fame but because she knows her presence is helping a lot of people. To feel that you are helpful, you are useful to society—this is happiness. When you have a path and you enjoy every step on your path, you are already someone. You don't need to become someone else. You already are what you want to become, practicing nonaction, the art of being.

When I was a young monk, I learned that the teachings of the Buddha could be summarized in four short sentences. People asked the Buddha how to be happy, and he said that all buddhas teach the same thing:

The bad things, don't do them.
The good things, try to do them.
Try to purify, subdue your own mind.
That is the teaching of all buddhas.*

I wasn't impressed. I thought to myself, "This is too simple. Everyone agrees that you have to do good things and refrain from doing bad things. To subdue and purify your mind is too vague." But after sixty-five years of practice I have a different perspective on this teaching. Looking carefully, I have seen that these four sentences are very meaningful.

---

*This translation is from the Chinese version of the Dhammapada.

Now I understand that the bad things you should avoid are those that create suffering for you and other people, including other living beings and the environment. Mindfulness helps you know whether something is a good thing or a bad thing, whether doing it will bring happiness or suffering to yourself and the people around you. When you refrain from doing bad things, you are practicing compassion, because you refrain from bringing suffering to yourself and other people. Practicing compassion is practicing happiness, because happiness is the absence of suffering. Then, try to do good things. Try to do whatever brings peace, stability, and joy to you and other people.

You practice love, you practice compassion, and you know that practicing love brings happiness. Happiness cannot exist without love. All the great spiritual teachers have told us to love, and the concrete means is to refrain from causing suffering and to offer happiness.

It is easy to say, easy to understand, but it is not always easy to do or to refrain from doing. Thus these first two things depend entirely on the third thing: to purify and subdue your mind. The mind is the ground of everything.

The Buddha said that all suffering comes from the mind but all happiness also comes from the mind. To purify your mind is to transform your way of perceiving things, to remove wrong perceptions. When you remove your wrong perceptions, you also remove your anger, your hate, your discrimination, and your craving.

Our minds can be intoxicated by three kinds of poison: the first is craving, the second is hate or violence, and the third is delusion. To purify your mind is to neutralize and transform these poisons in you. You neutralize these poisons with the three wisdoms, the energies of mindfulness, concentration, and insight.

If your mind is full of confusion, anger, and craving, then your mind is not pure, so even if you want to do good things you can't do them, and even if you want to refrain from doing bad things you cannot. You can offer happiness and refrain from causing suffering easily and beautifully only when you know how to subdue and purify your mind. This is the most special thing in Buddhism, the art of subduing and purifying your mind. Once our mind is subdued and transformed, happiness becomes possible.

When you walk from here to the pine tree, you begin with one step, and you can train yourself so that this step has within it the energy of mindfulness, concentration, and insight. If you really practice walking meditation, you will discover that every step you take generates the energies of mindfulness, concentration, and insight, bringing you a lot of happiness. When you walk like this, you are first aware that you are taking a step: that is the energy of mindfulness. I am here. I am alive. I am taking a step. You step and you know you are taking a step. That is mindfulness of walking. The mindfulness helps you be in the here and now, fully present, fully alive so that you can take the step. Zen Master Lin Chi said, "The miracle is not to walk on air, or on water, or on fire. The real miracle is to walk on earth." Walking with mindfulness, concentration, and insight is performing a miracle. You are truly alive. You are truly present, touching the wonders of life within you and around you.

We have invented many types of machines that save a lot of time. We can do wonders with a computer. A computer can work a hundred or a thousand times faster than a typewriter. In farming, it used to take several weeks to plough the fields; now you can do it in a few days. You don't have to wash your clothes by hand anymore—there's a washing machine. You don't have to go fetch the water, because the water comes to your kitchen. We have found many ways to save labor, and yet we are much busier than our ancestors were. That is a contradiction. Why is that? Because we have acquired so much and we are afraid of losing these things, so we have to work hard to keep them. That is why even if you have a lot, you still suffer and become depressed.

Manufacturers of medicine will tell you that the kinds of medicine we consume the most in our society—in tremendous quantities—are sedatives and antidepressants. When the Buddha talked about subduing and purifying our minds, he wasn't talking about sedation.

We have taken into ourselves so many toxins, poisons. The world we have created has overpowered us. We cannot escape anymore, even in our sleep. But peace and happiness are still available, once we see that the conditions we think are essential to our happiness may in fact bring us the opposite of happiness—depression, despair, and forgetfulness.

We have to begin with our breath. We have to breathe in mindfully to know that we are alive, that there are still wonders of life around us and in us that we can touch every minute for our transformation and healing. We have to use our feet to learn how to walk in the present, because each step will be transforming, healing, and nourishing.

Most of us walk like sleepwalkers. We walk, but we aren't there. We don't experience life or the wonders of life. There is little joy. We are sleepwalking through our own life, and our life is as unreal as a dream. Cultivating true power is about waking up from your dream. One mindful step can be a factor of awakening that brings you to life—that brings you the miracle of being alive. And when mindfulness is there, concentration is there, because mindfulness contains concentration. You can be less or more focused. You may be fifty, sixty, or ninety percent focused on your step, but the more focused you are, the better your chance of breaking through into insight. Mindfulness leads to concentration, which leads to insight. Insight is a fruit of our practice. Like an orange tree offers oranges, insight offers us the truths of impermanence, no-self, and interbeing.

Impermanence means that everything is changing, including the happiness you experience when you are doing walking meditation. Happiness, like all phenomena, is impermanent. It lasts for only one step; if the next step doesn't have mindfulness, concentration, and insight, then happiness will die. However, you know that you are capable of taking a second step that also generates the three energies of mindfulness, concentration, and insight, so you have the power to make happiness last longer. It's like when we ride a bicycle: we continue to pedal so that we can continue to move forward.

Happiness is impermanent, but it can be renewed. You are also impermanent and also renewable, like your breath, like your steps. You are not something permanent experiencing something impermanent. You are something impermanent experiencing something impermanent. If happiness can be renewed, so can you, because you in the next moment is a renewal of you in this moment. It's wonderful to know that happiness lasts only as long as one in-breath or one step, because we know we can renew our happiness in another breath or another step, provided we know the art of generating mindfulness, concentration, and insight.

The insight of impermanence leads to the insight of no-self. When we pursue individual happiness, our satisfaction is always ultimately fleeting, because individual happiness is not possible. Our happiness, our existence, is dependent on the existence and happiness of everyone and everything else. This is the insight of interbeing, the interconnectedness of all things. The father knows that if the son is not happy he himself cannot be truly happy, so when the father seeks his own happiness, he also seeks happiness for his son. Your mindful steps are not for you alone; they are for your partner and friends too, because the moment you stop suffering, others benefit.

When you take one mindful step, it might seem that you are taking a step for yourself alone. You are trying to find some peace, some stability, some happiness. But with insight, you see that everything good that you do for yourself, you are doing for all of us. If just one person in a family or a company practices, that practice will benefit everyone, not only the practitioner. When that person practices correctly, she gets the insight of no-self and she knows that she's doing it for everyone.

Perhaps you feel you are doing most of the work in your home or office. You get angry at others and feel they should be punished. When a feeling of anger or discrimination manifests, the practitioner recognizes that to allow such an energy to continue is not healthy for himself or for others. All these thoughts can be easily transformed once you have touched the nature of no-self. Practice mindfulness of breathing and walking in order to recognize the feeling of anger, to embrace the anger and transform it. When the element of ignorance is no longer there, the element of anger will be transformed. You don't transform it just for the benefit of others; you do it for yourself as well, because you see that there is no distinction between the two. With the insight of no-self, you no longer seek the kind of happiness that will make other people suffer. This kind of insight can liberate you and liberate the world.

So from here to the pine tree, I wish you good luck. Take a step in such a way that mindfulness, concentration, and insight can be generated, so that you get in touch with the here and now, you touch the wonders of life. Forget about the conditions of happiness that you have been running after for such a long time—money, power, wealth, sex—because you know that once you get them, you will still be unhappy. You want true life, true happiness, true power.

SIX

Boundless Love

When we are running around after our cravings and false power, we are missing out on something that is crucial to our happiness: the experience of love. With the insight of impermanence, no-self, and interbeing, we have the opportunity to experience true love. The French writer Antoine de Saint-Exupéry said that to love another doesn't mean we sit and look at each other; it means we both look in the same direction. We all should look deeply at our own lives to see whether in our experience this is true or not, and if it's true, to what degree. Each of us has needs and desires, so when we love someone, we have a natural tendency to look at him. We hope to see in him the goodness, truth, and beauty we are looking for. We are thirsting for sincerity. We are looking for something sacred, something beautiful, something good, and something wholesome. Many of us believe that once we find these qualities in another person, we will feel we don't lack anything, and we will be less alone.

We all start looking for the beautiful, the true, and the good in other people. Many of us believe there are only a few people who have these qualities. When we find these qualities in another person, we may fall in love with him because we believe we have discovered the essence of the true, beautiful, and good. We must be careful in this search, because we may have wrong perceptions. Sometimes the beauty we think is real is not true beauty. The truth we think is real is not real truth. And the wholesomeness we perceive is not real goodness. So we can love another based on a wrong perception. When we have gotten to know that person for a period of time, we discover that we have failed, because that person is not able to symbolize for us the beautiful, good, and true that we were looking for. We say that the person has deceived us, and we suffer. And then we go and look for someone else, another person to love. We may fail many times, falling into the same situation, growing tired of or disappointed with the other person. If we continue like this, we can spend our lives constantly looking for someone.

In the beginning, each of us feels that we lack something, that we are only half a person. And we wander around looking for our other half. We're like a saucepan without a lid, and we're always looking for our lid. We have an inferiority complex and believe that the true, the good, and the beautiful don't exist in us. This is a deep complex in every one of us. We have a perception that we are not worthy. We don't say these things—we may not even be consciously aware of them—but deep down we feel that we have no beauty, goodness, or truth.

Because we wish we had these things, we try to seem like we do, even if only on the outside. We want to show other people that we are good, that we are beautiful, even if only in appearance. In ourselves, we believe we are not really beautiful, not really good. And so we try to improve our appearance with cosmetics, clothes, diets, or plastic surgery. We want to appear more truthful and knowledgeable, so we look for things to study or unusual experiences that will bring us prestige. We adorn ourselves with titles and awards.

We are all deceiving each other. Deep down we feel there is nothing good, beautiful, and true in us, and at the same time we are desperate to show other people how good, beautiful, and truthful we are. And so we deceive ourselves from generation to generation. And while we are deceiving others, we are also being deceived by them. We are each other's victims. We are trying to make ourselves up so we will look less ugly, and others are doing the same.

Sitting at the foot of the bodhi tree on the night when he realized the truth, the Buddha discovered something that was very surprising to him and also to us. He saw that the good, the beautiful, and the true are to be found in everyone, but very few people know that. People think that the true, the beautiful, and the good exist somewhere else, in someone else. They don't know that they are true, beautiful, and good at their core. Our whole life, we are looking for someone else to replace what we feel is missing.

This is what the Buddha said at the moment of enlighten-ment: "How strange—all living beings have the fully awakened nature, but none of them knows it. And because of that they drift and sink from lifetime to lifetime in the great ocean of *samsara*, in suffering."

When we recognize that in us there is the essence of good-ness, beauty, and truth, we will stop going in search of some-thing. We will stop wandering around feeling that we lack something. And we are able to stop deceiving others. We don't have to adorn ourselves because we have discovered the true, the beautiful, and the good here within us.

We are like an ocean wave that believes it is fragile and ugly and that the other waves are more beautiful, more powerful. The wave has an inferiority complex. But when this wave gets in touch with its true nature, water, it sees that water goes beyond all concepts of beautiful, ugly, high, low, here, and there. Whether it's a large wave or a small wave, half a wave or a third of a wave, it is still made out of water. Water is beyond all these qualifications—it is without birth and without death. A wave is really only water, and as far as water is concerned, all waves are equal because all waves are water.

Everyone who lives in this world—women, men, rich, poor, educated, uneducated,sick, healthy—they all have this basis of goodness, beauty, and truth. Don't go looking outside yourself anymore, because the thing you are looking for is already there within you. All living beings have the pure, clear, complete nature within themselves. And everyone has to return to herself to be in touch properly with that beautiful, good, and true that is within her. When you have been in touch with this inner nature, you will put an end to the many lifetimes of searching and have a steadfast faith in yourself. Then you will have happiness; you will have peace.

The Buddha said we each have beauty within us, but this may be hard to accept if in our home, our community, and our workplace we're getting a different message. Many of us believe our workplace is not a safe place. Often at work, we are afraid of disapproval. We are afraid to be ourselves, and we change who we are to be accepted. If your happiness depends entirely on the views of other people, you have no confidence in yourself. Then, when you are not recognized by others as beautiful and worthy, you suffer. This is what makes you want to be someone else, something else, which is the foundation of suffering.

A flower doesn't have this kind of fear. It stands in a garden with many other kinds of flowers, some pink or yellow, some with many petals, others with just a few. But a flower never tries to imitate another flower. Don't try to be someone else. You don't need plastic surgery. The cosmos has come together and helped you manifest in this way, and you are beautiful just as you are. To be beautiful means to be yourself. You don't need to be accepted by others. You need to accept yourself. When you are born a lotus flower, be beautiful as a lotus flower; don't try to be a magnolia flower. If you crave acceptance and recognition and try to change yourself to fit what other people want you to be, you will suffer all your life. True happiness and true power lie in understanding yourself, accepting yourself, having confidence in yourself.

There was a young man who came to Plum Village to become a monk. He had many difficulties because he craved recognition for his good looks and his talent. His whole life he was looking for acceptance from other people. He thought he would find it as a monk, but he still suffered. If three or four monks were sharing joyfully and communicating well, when that young monk tried to join in, the atmosphere of joy stopped. It wasn't because they tried to exclude him. His energy of demanding recognition dominated the environment and made it difficult for others to be joyful around him.

One day I called him in and said, "Your seeking recognition is causing you suffering. You may want to experiment with being yourself and coming to others without the need to be recognized. If you practice mindfulness to see the suffering and the needs of other people in the community, the need to be recognized will not be so strong in you anymore. When you approach others like that, people will accept you much more easily. And if you really have beautiful qualities and talents, they will recognize them."

At first the monk resisted this. So many years of seeking were hard to change. But slowly, he began to have moments when he forgot to seek and demand. Happiness crept up on him.

We have ideas about what beauty is, about what we value, and these ideas may be obstacles to our happiness. We imagine things, we construct things in our mind, and we suffer because of it. We are afraid people are judging us, and it is this fear, rather than the actual judgment, that upsets us. The suffering is created entirely in our own minds.

The practice of love as taught by the Buddha is very clear. It involves cultivating the equanimity that comes from the insight of no-self. When we understand that every thing is made of everything else, we stop searching for the perfect partner or for individual recognition. We can learn to look in this way when we look at another person and when we look at ourselves. Everything that manifests itself in this world is a wonder. Practicing seeing things through these eyes can help us see ourselves as wonders of life.

There are occasions when the lack of understanding between you and another is really there. You may be misunderstood by many people, and yet you don't have to suffer. Just live your life properly and, after a while, others will correct their misperception of you. You know what is going on inside you. You know how your mind is. If every day you produce positive thinking, good ideas, with understanding and compassion; if every day you practice loving speech; if every day you do good actions, you know it yourself. Your value will reveal itself to the people around you. It may take a few days or several weeks, it may even take years. But if you know who you are, you don't have to suffer anymore. The practice of understanding yourself and training yourself to produce more and more beautiful thoughts, words, and actions gives you self-confidence, and that will transform everything else.

Remember that the first spiritual power is faith. The Buddha, or any of the other great spiritual teachers, didn't want us to be slaves, dependent on someone else for our confidence. He didn't want people to lean on him. He was very clear: "You have what you are looking for within yourself." In our own nature, there is a teacher we can turn to and take refuge in. You can have faith in the basic goodness, the basic beauty, and the basic truth that is in you. You have to go back to yourself and discover it. It is your own ground of being. It is the basis of your true power.

When we look at the person we love, we can look at him with this understanding. We can say to our beloved, "Let's not live in this narrow way anymore. Let's both return to our own basis. Let's not deceive each other anymore. We don't need to deceive each other, because the thing we are looking for is already there in us." Then you become friends on the spiritual path, a path that leads us not on an outer search but on an inner one.

When we love someone, we feel strong, we feel powerful. We feel happy because we have found a companion who can understand us. That energy is pure and beautiful. But we need to take care of that energy with mindfulness. If we don't know how to take care of our love, it can easily turn into suffering. When understanding is there, we know what to do and what not to do to bring happiness and peace to the other person. This is true love. We nourish our understanding by practicing deep listening and loving speech. Without true love, you can't be happy at all.

When you fall in love without the five spiritual powers, you risk depending on the other person's beauty or goodness instead of your own. But if you have mindfulness and concentration, you know how to handle your love, and the love will not create suffering in you and your beloved. Love is an energy. Is it giving rise to more craving, to more anxiety and fear? Or does it give us the energy of peace, of compassion and liberation? In Buddhism we are encouraged to love every living being as a mother loves her only child; this is called boundless love. It is a tremendous source of energy. With the power of mindfulness, of concentration and insight, we can transform our limited love into a source of boundless love.

The Buddha spoke about four elements that constitute true love: the capacity to be kind and offer happiness, *maitri* in Sanskrit; compassion, the capacity to relieve suffering, *karuna*; the capacity to bring joy every day, *mudita*; and finally, the capacity of nondiscrimination, *upeksha*. When there is true love, there is nondiscrimination. The pain of the other is our own pain; the happiness of the other is our own happiness. In the light of nondiscrimination, happiness and pain are collective and not individual. If we do not understand our partner, if we do not share in her suffering, this is not love at all; it's just consuming the other person to satisfy our own individual needs. True love is characterized by attentiveness, respect. If we have this attention, then when we see the suffering of the other person, we can't go on causing them pain. If we have respect, we cannot go on like that.

To make our love meaningful, we need to nourish our bodhicitta, our mind of boundless love and compassion. Our limited love actually can help us. One relationship can be a foundation for gaining more insight into our situation and the situation of the world. We can cultivate in ourselves the five spiritual powers of faith, diligence, mindfulness, concentration, and in-sight, and we can support our beloved in cultivating her powers. First, we learn to love one person with all our under-standing and insight, then we expand that love to embrace an-other person, and another, until our love is truly boundless.

When we meditate, we look deeply to nourish our joy and peace, and to embrace our suffering and transform it into wisdom and liberation. Love is no different from meditation. It is what we do with our love that makes it into a spiritual power. Our aim is to transform our limited love into true love, bound-less love, offering ourselves and others the great gifts of com-passion, transformation, and healing.

Ananda was the Buddha's cousin. One day he went on an alms round to receive offerings of food. He stopped at a well to ask for some water because he was thirsty. Sitting by the well was a young woman called Matanga. She was a *dalit*, a member of what was called, at that time, the untouchable caste. The higher castes would not touch or come near them because they believed the untouchables would pollute them. So when Ananda asked for water, she said, "No, I can't give it to you because I am an untouchable and I will pollute you." Ananda said, "In our teaching, there is no caste division. The Buddha has told us that we are all equal, therefore you can give me water. I won't be polluted, so don't be afraid." Matanga was very happy. She lifted the water with a ladle and gave it to him to drink. He joined his palms, thanked her, and went home.

Matanga fell in love with Ananda. She couldn't sleep, she couldn't eat, because she kept thinking about how beautiful, good, and kind he was. When her mother saw that her daughter couldn't sleep or eat for many weeks, she wanted to help her.

So one day they met Ananda as he was going on an alms round, and they invited him to come to their house so they could make offerings. When he came in, they gave him a bowl of tea made from an herb that took away his clarity. As soon as Ananda drank the tea, he knew something felt wrong, and he didn't know how to put it right. He knew he was in a dangerous situation, so he began to practice meditation. He didn't say anything, he didn't do anything. He sat in the cross-legged position and began to follow his breathing.

The Buddha, who was in the Jeta Grove, wondered why Ananda had not returned. So he asked two other monks to go and look for Ananda. They found Ananda sitting in meditation in Matanga's house and led him back to the Jeta Grove Monastery. Matanga was weeping so hard that they also brought her back to the monastery. By the time Ananda came back to the monastery, the effect of the tea was wearing off, and he prostrated himself before the Buddha and thanked him for helping him return.

Then Matanga came in. The Buddha asked Matanga to sit down. He said, "Do you love Ananda that much?" And Matanga said, "Yes, I love him very much." And the Buddha said, "What do you love in Ananda? Do you love his eyes? His nose?"

Matanga replied, "I love his eyes, I love his nose, I love his ears, I love his mouth. I love everything about Ananda. I think I cannot live if I don't have Ananda."

The Buddha said, "There are many things in Ananda that you haven't seen and that you would love even more if you could see them."

"Like what?" she asked.

The Buddha smiled and said, "Like Ananda's love, like Ananda's bodhicitta. All you've seen is eyes, nose, ears, mouth. As a young man, he gave up his life in a wealthy family to become a monk, with the aim of helping many people. Ananda could never be happy with one or two people, because that happiness is so small. That is why he became a monk. He wants to be able to help many, many people. He has a mind of great equality. He wants to love but not just one person. He wants to love thousands and thousands of people. Ananda's bodhicitta is very beautiful. If only you could see it, you would love Ananda even more.

"If you really love Ananda, you can help him realize his deep aspiration as a monk, help him realize his bodhicitta. Ananda is like a cool breeze. If you want to possess it and lock it in a small box, you will lose this refreshing cool breeze. Ananda is like a cloud floating in the blue sky, very beautiful. If you want to catch the cloud and put it in a box and turn the key, then you will kill Ananda, because you haven't seen the most beautiful things about him. If you were to see them, you would love him more, and you would love him in a way that would help him be Ananda, just as you can help a cloud be a cloud floating in the beautiful blue sky.

"Don't think that Ananda is the only one who has that beautiful aspiration. You are the same. You have that beauty, too.

You can also live like Ananda, if you really love Ananda and you are able to see his bodhicitta. You will be able to return to yourself and see that you have bodhicitta in yourself, and you can vow to Ananda that you too will live in such a way as to make as many people happy as possible."

When Matanga heard this, she was surprised. She said, "I don't have any worth. I belong to the lowest caste. I can't make anybody happy." The Buddha said, "Yes, you have already done it. You already have the beautiful, good, and true in you. Everyone has that. And if we return to ourselves, and we are able to be in touch with that basic goodness, truth, and beauty in us, we will have faith in it, and we will know that we can bring happiness to many people."

Matanga asked, "Is that really so? Can I really leave the family life, become a nun, and help thousands of people like Ananda?" And the Buddha said, "Yes, why not? If you can be in touch with the true, good, and beautiful in you, and give rise to bodhicitta, you will be like Ananda and bring happiness to many people." Her insight was opened by the Buddha, and she touched the earth before him. She became a nun so that her love could open up and become measureless.

Also in the time of the Buddha, there was a monk named Vaikali. He became attached to the Buddha, but his love was superficial. He saw the Buddha as a realm of light. When he sat near the Buddha, he felt very happy, and that's all he wanted. He felt so peaceful, so happy, so content sitting by the Buddha. He didn't listen deeply or carefully to the dharma talks. He just spent his time gazing at the Buddha. But even though he was staring right at the Buddha, he could see only his shadow; he could see only the small beauty of the Buddha. He didn't see the great wisdom, the great love of the Buddha. Wherever he was, he just wanted to be with the Buddha. Wherever he sat, he just wanted to sit near the Buddha.

After a time, the Buddha saw that Vaikali was still very weak. So the Buddha decided he wouldn't allow Vaikali to be near him anymore. He would not allow him to be his attendant. Vaikali thought the Buddha had abandoned him and didn't love him anymore. Vaikali wanted to kill himself. The Buddha knew this was happening, so he tried to find a way to save him. The Buddha came and asked, "What are you doing?" He helped Vaikali see that his love wasn't the deep love of a monk but a superficial attachment. The Buddha showed him that in his own self, deep down, there was the beautiful, the good, and the true, and he should be looking for that instead of chasing after an image of the good, beautiful, and true outside him.

At first, people are infatuated with an image they see as beautiful. They want to possess this image, and they suffer because of this. But after they wake up and see that it is a deception, they push away this image to look for another object of infatuation. They may wander their whole lives, from lifetime to lifetime, unable to find the real object of their love. But if we can find someone who has a steady faith in her own goodness, beauty, and truth, we can look at this person as a reflection of ourselves in order to return to ourselves and be in touch with the basic goodness, beauty, and truth in us. Then we will be happy, we will be able to put an end to our wandering. We can become someone who loves all beings, not just one person. We become someone who serves others. That is all the Buddha did in his life—rescue and love other beings.

A good spiritual teacher can show us that in our own heart we also have a spiritual teacher and we have to take refuge in this teacher inside us rather than becoming attached to a teacher outside us, because the spiritual teacher outside may be a fake. A true teacher will always encourage us to be in touch with the teacher within us. If we take refuge in this teacher within us, we will never be disappointed. If a wave has faith in its nature of water, the wave will never be disappointed.

Just as our true teacher is within us, the real object of our love is ourselves. We have to know how to love ourselves, how to return to our true nature, to see the wholesome, the good, the true, and the beautiful within us. Then we will be able to see it in others When we have seen real beauty, goodness, and truth in ourselves and others, we will no longer be deceived by outer displays When we love someone, we have the duty to look at that person in such a way that our vision is not obscured by wrong perceptions. True goodness contains true beauty and authentic truth. This is the insight of interbeing. Truth is always beautiful. Kindness is always beautiful. And beauty is always true and kind.

Together with our beloved, we can practice being in touch with the beauty, goodness, and truth within us, so that we can help ourselves and numberless others. This is the path of the Buddha. Whether we are nun or monk, wife or husband, girlfriend or boyfriend, we have to stop deceiving ourselves and others, and allowing others to deceive us. The great awakening occurs when we recognize that what we are looking for is within us. Then our suffering will end and we will be happy.

SEVEN

Being Present at Home and at Work

Once you have seen the truth and beauty within yourself, then you can see it within your loved one. To love means being there for your beloved, recognizing his presence as important. To be there, to be fully present, to appreciate the preciousness of your beloved, this is the practice of true love. To be there for him, you have to be there for yourself first. Do you have the time to be there for yourself? Do you have the time for a cup of tea, for an orange, for your in-breath, your out-breath? Do you have the time to take steps without thinking of your projects?

If you don't understand yourself, if you are not capable of accepting yourself, it will be impossible for you to understand and accept the other person. The practice of mindfulness will help you get deeply in touch with yourself, so that you can understand your suffering, your difficulties, your deepest aspiration.

First of all, there may be a lack of communication within you. Your body and your consciousness have been trying to tell you many things, but you may not have time to listen. Your liver may be under great stress, but you continue to drink alcohol. Your body may be begging you to slow down or take a day of rest, but you keep pushing it and working harder.

You may not be there for your own body, you may not care enough about your own body or know how to listen to it. There may be blocks of pain in your consciousness, but you don't know how to listen to your consciousness.

The first step in loving communication is for you to go home to yourself. You take the royal way back to yourself through mindful breathing to touch the joy, the beauty, the wonders of life in and around you. The practice of being mindful of your breathing, your walking, your breakfast-making helps you go home to yourself in the here and now, to be mindful of what is going on in your body, your feelings and your perceptions, to recognize and transform your suffering.

If anger is coming up, you become aware of your anger. If fear is coming up, you become aware of your fear. You are always there for yourself. "Good morning, my little anger, I know you are there. I will take good care of you." "Good afternoon, my fear, you just manifested. I know you are always there, you are my old friend. I will take time to care for you." Then you practice walking mindfully, breathing mindfully, acknowledging the presence of your fear or your anger and soothing it.

Self-understanding and self-love provide the foundation for understanding and loving another person. This is the first step: going home to ourselves, taking care of ourselves, understanding ourselves, accepting ourselves, and being compassionate to ourselves.

The most precious gift you can make to your loved one is not money, power, or fame, but your true presence. To love means to be present for him. How can you love if you are not there? And the quality of your presence is very important. You have to be there, fresh, loving, understanding. Through the practice of mindful breathing and mindful walking, you bring your mind back to your body, you establish yourself in the here and now, you are fully present, and you can go to your loved one and say the first declaration of love, "Darling, you know, I am really here for you."

You don't need to bring anything else; you just offer your presence. And your presence, thanks to the understanding and compassion generated by your practice, can be fresh, nourishing, and healing to her.

I know an eleven-year-old boy named Tim. The day before his birthday, his father said to him, "Tomorrow is your birthday. Tell me what you'd like and I'll buy it for you." This made Tim unhappy. He knew that his father was rich and could afford to buy him anything. But Tim didn't want anything. He didn't need more things. He needed just one thing, which he had found very difficult to obtain, and that was the presence of his father. His father was rarely home, and even when he was home, he wasn't really there. He might be sitting there at home, but only his body was there. His mind was absorbed in other things. So to Tim it was like he didn't have a father. So he said, "Daddy, I want you. I don't want anything else. I just want you."

What could the father do? He knew his son needed his true presence. He began to practice mindful breathing to be present for himself so that he could be present for his son. He didn't do it in time for his son's birthday. But about a month later, he went up to his son's room, held his son's hand, and said, "Son, now I am really here for you." This true presence can't be bought in the market. It is the deep practice of mindfulness.

"Darling, I am really here for you" is the most meaningful declaration of love. It is not a mere statement; it is a practice. If you are not there and just pretend to be present, the other person will know. You may be possessed by your projects, your worries, your fear, and you pretend to be there but are not really there. Only with practice can you produce your true presence. Your loved one needs your true presence and nothing less. "Darling, I am here for you." When we say this, we recognize the precious presence of our beloved. If we don't recognize his presence, it's like he doesn't exist at all. Without our attention and mindfulness, the other person doesn't feel loved.

You might be driving, with your beloved sitting very close to you, close enough to touch. If you are entirely absorbed by your projects, fear, worries, and thinking, you neglect her completely. You alienate her because your mind has no space for her. And if you continue to live like that, her happiness will soon die, because she feels like she's not loved, she doesn't have your attention, your mindfulness. It is important to go home to yourself through mindful breathing from time to time, so you can look at her and say, "Darling, I know you are there and it makes me happy." This is the second declaration of love. It is very simple. You embrace her with the energy of mindfulness. Embraced by your energy of mindfulness, your beloved will be very happy and will bloom like a flower.

If you know the techniques of mindful breathing and mindful walking, you can be there for your loved ones in just one or two minutes. In my hermitage in France, in the early morning when I walk to the meditation hall, I go down a path with many trees. Passing the trees, I look up and see the full or half moon. I have a habit of looking at the moon and smiling to it, and I practice, "Dear moon, I know you are there, and I am very happy." You may practice the same with your beloved. Breathe in and out mindfully, smile, and become fully alive, fully present, then go to your beloved, look into her eyes, and say, "Darling, I know you are there, alive, and this makes me very happy." This is the act of recognizing the presence of your beloved. It's not difficult. Everyone can do it with a little practice in mindful breathing and walking.

Because you are fully present, you may notice that the voice of your beloved carries some pain or sorrow. Mindfulness helps us know what is going on in our beloved. With the practice of mindful breathing and mindful walking, you become fully present and use the third declaration of love: "Darling, I know that you suffer. That's why I am here for you."

Before you can do anything for your loved one, just practicing saying these words will bring a huge relief. When you suffer and your loved one doesn't know about it, you suffer even more. But if he knows, you suffer much less right away. These declarations of love are a miracle that you can produce by the practice of mindfulness. "Darling, I am really here for you. Darling, I know that you are there and I'm very happy. Darling, I know you suffer; that is why I am here for you." Practicing offering your true presence to yourself and to him is something you can do every day.

Because you are able to go home to yourself to restore harmony, acceptance, and peace within, not only can you practice these three declarations of love, but with your improved quality of being, you can also help your beloved go home to herself and do for herself what you have done. You now have the energy of mindfulness and concentration. You are able to handle your body and your feelings. Now you can begin to help your loved ones do the same. That's the second step. You can help her yourself or you can borrow the energy of your community to help you do it. If you belong to a community of practice, a church or group where people know the practice of mindfulness, it's much easier. Your brothers and sisters in the community support you. This gives you enough mindfulness and concentration to go home to yourself, and you can help your partner do the same. When your practice is strong, your partner becomes your ally, not only in the practice, but also in your work of serving people. You are copractitioners. You are on the same spiritual path. And both of you are stronger.

When you are united as partners, whether father and son, husband and wife, or close friends, you bring this foundation of understanding and support into your business, into your professional life, because healthy relationships in your private life are the ground of all other success.

In your professional life, there may be other people you have to be in touch with and work with. You may be working as a team to make a film, design a product, or complete another kind of project. Each person on your team has his own difficulties, his own suffering. But because you are open, happy, fresh, and concentrated, you can help all of them touch their freshness. You don't care only about their work performance, because the quality of their work depends on the peace and well-being inside of each of them. You come to the business as a friend, helping everyone transform, bringing peace, harmony, and well-being into their lives at home and at work.

It is important to share with them—but skillfully—your practice of mindfulness, because the people who work with you all share the same ideal of service as you do. Even if they are talented and do their jobs well, you still need them to share your concerns, your insight. You have to treat people at work—other employees, members of your staff, and people in different companies with whom you interact—the same way you treat your partner. There should be mutual understanding, support, and compassion. Your co-workers should feel comfortable contributing their insight to you and vice versa. This is crucial, if you want to be successful and serve your customers or your constituents well.

No matter how busy you are, take the time to inquire about each co-worker's situation—their families, their difficulties. Use loving speech and deep listening to inspire confidence, so that people have a chance to speak out and tell you the truth. There may be conflicts in your company that you don't know about because you have been so busy. If you don't know what's going on, you'll make mistakes. When you know better what is going on, you can respond in a way that will help transform the problems and get things on the right track, making your organization more effective.

There need to be people in your company who have the capacity to understand, to listen attentively to the concerns of your staff. You can ask them to look deeply into the situation of the people in your company and report to you the suffering that exists. This is the practice of loving speech and deep listening, which can restore communication.

When you focus on only the shortcomings in another person, you aren't capable of seeing their good qualities. Everyone has both strengths and weaknesses. When you see only what's wrong in another person, when you aren't capable of seeing her good qualities, something is wrong with your perception. When you have wrong perceptions of others, it means you don't have correct perceptions of yourself, you don't know what your own strengths and weaknesses are.

The solution to this is to learn to look more deeply. That is real meditation. Meditation is the art of looking deeply. If you want to look deeply, you have to train yourself in mindfulness and concentration. When you're aware and realize that time is quickly passing by, you make the effort to learn how to live each moment deeply in order to make your life more meaningful. You'll know what to do and what not to do to improve the quality of your own life and the lives of the people around you.

When you feel stressed out at work, you know that you are experiencing ill-being. With all your intelligence, compassion, and goodwill, you can help create work conditions that don't cause your co-workers to become victims of stress. We have a habit of trying to work more efficiently, and we associate this with working fast, but we need to rethink this. If we realize that doing our work with mindfulness actually requires no more time than doing it unmindfully, a lot of our stress disappears. We need to practice so that we work in happiness, freedom, and solidity—so that everything we do, even cleaning, washing, and cooking, is done in happiness, solidity, and freedom Otherwise our time is wasted.

But if you're not capable of understanding this for yourself or your family, you won't be able to do it for your co-workers. If you're not able to enjoy relaxation and you can't help members of your family enjoy moments of relaxation, how can you help your employees enjoy relaxation? If you don't take care of your family, how can you expect your employees to take care of their families? And if their families are a mess, how can they be happy and productive at work? Anything you can do for yourself and your family is at the same time taking care of the people at work.

Remember the insight of interbeing. Co-workers and employees are made of noncoworker, nonemployee elements: society, family, and so on. You need to listen compassionately so your employees can talk to you about their families. When you really care, you become a friend and not just a moneymaker. You act out of generosity and compassion, supporting not only your colleagues but your business, giving it a greater chance of success.

When a difficult situation arises, many of us react right away. And we often act as if the other person or group were our enemy, especially at work. We don't treat others as brothers and sisters whom we have to help, and our actions create more division. It's important to interact with people in a genuinely nonviolent way.

Loving speech and deep listening are so important. We have to show our understanding. What the other person did or said may have been a result of their lack of insight and understanding. Punishing them will make the situation only worse. If something goes wrong in a company, our first instinct is to find out whose fault it is and punish them. But to understand them is far more effective. When you're able to understand, you'll have compassion, and you'll be able to accept them and find means to help them. I suggest we learn to look at people with whom we are having difficulties as people who can teach us, not people for us to punish.

We should consider each other fellow travelers sitting in the same boat. If the boat sinks, we will all sink together. When you create the understanding that the company is a boat carrying all, everyone will feel responsibility for the company and contribute the best of his abilities.

If you understand your employees, you will be able to love, accept, and care for them. You want more than employees; you want allies, allies on the path of service. This is possible. In Plum Village, where I live, there are a few hundred nuns, monks, and laypersons, and each of us comes from a different environment, a different culture. We belong to many nationalities, and yet it is possible for us to live as a big family, because we know the practice of reconciliation, the practice of accepting and loving each other. Because we know how to live simply and happily, we have enough time to open our doors and receive the many people who come to learn the practice of healing, transformation, and reconciliation.

Once we have created good communication and harmony in our workplace, we can extend it to our customers or constituents, and finally to the larger community. This is the final step. We should maintain ongoing communication with those we serve, whether they are people who have voted us into political office, stockholders of our company, or patients in our hospital. Dialogue should be open, so all feel they can express their suffering. This is already a great relief. Even if you have not been able to do anything yet to alleviate the problems, just listening and showing that you understand inspires confidence. You let them know that you have understood them, that you are trying to do something to eradicate the causes of the suffering. Good communication between you and the people you serve is crucial. By listening deeply to them, you will be able to understand the nature of their suffering and you will have insight into how to transform the situation.

If you are a politician, you also need to practice deep listening, whether in city hall, the state capitol, or Congress, so that you can profit from the insight of other elected officials. All elected officials have insights to share. Just because they belong to a different political party doesn't mean that they have nothing valuable to contribute. We all lose when we think that everything people in our party do and say is right and everything people in another party do and say is wrong. This is simply not true. If we think, speak, and act only along party lines, we operate like a machine without insight, without understanding, without compassion. We should be led by our understanding, our insight, and the collective understanding and insight we receive from our workplace and the people who have voted for us.

We are not elected to Congress to fight only for our ideas. Your idea may be superb, but it might still be improved by the ideas of other people. Regardless of what party a person belongs to, if she has a real insight, we should practice deep listening to really hear her. If she is fighting only for her own idea we will know it clearly, but if she has a real insight we must be open to it. Listening in this way will help Congress become a community where there is mutual understanding, mutual sharing. Our democracy will be safer. The integrity of the individual and the integrity of our institutions will be saved; otherwise there is only the appearance of democracy, not real democracy. When you are not yourself, when you are not operating on the ground of your insight, your compassion, your experience, when you have to speak and vote solely along party lines, you are not truly yourself, you are not offering your best to your nation and your people. The aspiration to offer our best is there in each of us. We should help each other be our best, because only then can we truly serve our people and our nation.

Just as politicians need to collaborate with those in opposing political parties, businesspeople can learn to collaborate with and learn from other companies rather than competing with them. Communication is important, not just within a company but between companies. It is possible to replace competition with cooperation and collaboration. If the leaders of corporations get together and practice looking deeply into the situation of the world to develop the products that best serve society, they will be able to devise mutually beneficial policies and working conditions. If they become sensitive to the suffering of humankind and the suffering of other species, they'll be able to come together without fighting.

When there is mutual understanding and sharing of insight, we will continue to have the support of those we serve; there is no doubt about this. We will feel much more supported and joyful in our work. This is true between you and your partner, between you and people in your office, and between you and the people you serve. If you are handling the present moment well, with all your wisdom and compassion, there is no need to worry about the future, because the future is made of only the present moment.

It is important to learn how to get other people to take care of things that you think you alone can do. Even a Buddhist teacher has to practice that. She has to look around to identify people who can help her. She can't do everything by herself, and by getting help she gives others a chance to emerge as teachers. She may be surprised to see that among her students there are those who can do things like teaching or taking care of the community better than she can herself.

So please don't give yourself the idea that you're irreplaceable. You must delegate your tasks to others, even if in the beginning you don't think they're as good as you are. You can support them with your happiness and your freshness. Together you can transform your workplace into a dynamic force that can change our society.

If you are used to the world of business, you may wonder how mindfulness fits in. If we are constantly focused on living in the present moment, how can we get things done?

To dwell in the here and now does not mean you never think about the past or responsibly plan for the future. The idea is simply not to allow yourself to get lost in regrets about the past or worries about the future. If you are firmly grounded in the present moment, the past can be an object of inquiry, the object of your mindfulness and concentration. You can attain many insights by looking into the past. But you are still grounded in the present moment.

The past is still there in the present. Both the happiness and the suffering you have experienced in the past are still there, alive, in the present moment. In the past, you may have made mistakes, you may have been unskillful and caused suffering to yourself and your beloved. People say it is impossible to go back to the past to fix our mistakes. But with mindfulness it is possible to go back and repair the damage, because the past is available in the present moment. Suppose you said something unkind to your grandmother and made her suffer, and now you regret it because she has passed away and you can't apologize to her. If you look deeply, your grandmother is always alive in you, in every cell of your body. As you breathe in, you can say, "Grandmother, I know you are there in every cell of my body," and breathing out, "I'm sorry." You decide to be kinder and more aware of your beloved ones now. Then you will see your grandmother smiling to you, and your wound will heal. This practice is wonderful because the past is still available to you. If you look deeply into it, you can learn a lot from the past and heal wounds from the past. Mindfulness of the past is very different from getting carried away in sorrow and regret.

In the same way, while you are grounded in the present moment, you can bring the future into the present as an object of inquiry, and you may have many insights. But insight and looking deeply are different from being distracted by fear and uncertainty about the future. If you allow yourself to be worried and afraid of the future, you lose time and waste your life. When you worry about success in the future and become obsessed with it, your thinking is not productive. To be anxious about the future does not help. The fact is that the future is made of the present. If you take care of the present to the best of your ability, you are doing everything you can to ensure a happy future. When you waste your energy in fear, stress, despair, and worry, you are spoiling both the present and the future.

You have the right to plan your future, but you have to let go first and put your anchor down in the present. You must dwell in the present to effectively plan for the future. Your only worry should be to sit stably in the present moment in order to skillfully take care of the future.

If we continue to be overwhelmed by our worries and harassed by stress and fear, tension will accumulate day after day and cause all sorts of diseases. Worries, suffering, and agitation cause tension in our bodies and bring stress to our minds, leading to conflicts in our families and our workplaces. Stress and tension can cause our thinking to become violent. Coming back to the present moment to take care of ourselves, to heal the tension and pain we may be suppressing, means that we suffer less and become happier. We get in touch with what's fresh, what's wonderful, what has the capacity to heal us. So coming back to the present moment actually gives us the strength we need to continue on into the future. When we are happy, and our loved ones are happy, it's easy to plan for and take care of the future.

If we don't know how to do this but keep obsessing about the future, our thinking won't bring us much benefit. We don't really need to think a whole lot. If we are healthy, light, happy, and fresh, our thinking is creative. New ideas come to us easily. If day after day our mind is burdened by worries, fears, and suffering, negative thoughts arise and we don't have enough clarity to take care of our families and our work.

We breathe in and become aware of our body. We breathe out and relax all the tension inside. When we drive, we can breathe at every red light. While waiting for the elevator or in line at the grocery store, we can practice relaxing our body; this is beneficial for our success in the future. We need only one or two really good ideas to become successful in our profession. People around us may have a lot ambition and drive, but because they don't know how to live in the present moment, they lack creativity, the power of insight, and the power to cut off their afflictions. But when we practice mindfulness in our daily life, we can hit our target in just one try. You can hit your target only when there's clarity in your mind, when there's concentration.

When we live in the present moment and walk, breathe, and take care of ourselves and our loved ones, our mindfulness and concentration increase each day. Mindfulness means we know what's going on. If our mind is filled with worry and tension, we recognize the worry and tension and breathe with them. When we look deeply into them, we see their roots. With the power of insight, we will see how to easily resolve our problems.

In this present moment I care that my thinking be the right kind of thinking, thinking that reflects understanding and compassion. This kind of thinking can nourish and transform me, bringing joy and happiness to me and people around me. In this very moment, I care that my speech be the kind of speech that communicates understanding and compassion, the kind of speech that can restore communication and offer confidence and reconciliation. At this very moment, I care about my physical action. My physical action should be able to translate my understanding and my compassion. If I'm sure that my thinking, speech, and physical action are in line with understanding and compassion, I don't have to worry anymore about the future, and I save a lot of energy. I want to invest one hundred percent of myself into the present moment. And this is possible. If I know I am doing my best in the present moment, I'm not afraid of the views or ideas of people now and in the future. The past, the present, and the future are interconnected. The present contains both the past and the future.

If you are a politician and you can practice this, you don't have to worry about whether you'll be reelected. If you are a businessperson and you practice like this, you don't have to worry about your next promotion. If you know exactly what you must do in the present moment, if you know how to take care of yourself and your loved ones, then you're doing everything you can do to take care of the present moment. You can be at peace. You don't have to worry about the future at all. It is possible to cultivate the elements of peace, joy, and well-being in ourselves by living deeply every moment of our daily life. If we do this, we don't need to worry about the future. Despair and anxiety cannot afflict us if we know that we are already taking care of the present moment the best way we can. What more is there to worry about?

Sometimes people worry about the future because they want to be as successful as they were in the past. When you create something that is well received, that becomes a hit, you are happy about your success. If you write a book that sells one million copies, you're happy and you want your next book to be equally popular. If it isn't, you suffer. If you're a film producer and you succeed in making a film that is highly acclaimed and popular, you care very much that your next film will also do well. If the next film is not as successful, you suffer. The same is true in politics, business, sports, and other professions where success is concerned. I have learned a great deal from this, and I am convinced that the most important thing is to have confidence in your work, to make sure that your work embodies your best, in terms of understanding and compassion. Maybe one hundred years from now a person or group will recognize your work. You don't need to be recognized right here and right now. If you see this, you don't have to suffer.

To me, a masterpiece should contain insight, understanding, and compassion. When I write a poem or a short story, what I care about most is doing my best. Whether people approve of it or not, whether it is a success or not, is not important to me. The most important thing for me is that I do the best I can. I care very much that the work embody my insight and compassion.

When you are filled with understanding and compassion, you have plenty of energy to serve, you are fully alive, very active, and your work, your film, your story, your novel, your poem is an expression of that mind of awakening. And it brings you great satisfaction to know that your work contains understanding and compassion. Even if people are not eager to buy it, you don't feel depressed at all, because you know the value of your work. You know that sooner or later someone will see the value of your work and he will be able to profit from it, provided that your work is a real work of art, carrying within itself the power of awakening, understanding, and compassion.

When Van Gogh was alive, his work wasn't appreciated. But that doesn't mean his work didn't have tremendous value. My book *Anger* sold one million copies in South Korea alone, and they called it a hit. Recently I published a very small book called *Touching the Earth*. Only two or three thousand copies were printed. But I am not eager to sell a million copies. I know that a number of monks, nuns, and laypersons are using it to practice, to transform their suffering. And I know the book will serve many generations of practitioners in the future. I don't need it to be a hit. I need to believe that it is a good book, a good manual for practice, and that already satisfies me completely. My happiness is not dependent on popularity, on others' approval. My happiness depends on me. If you can go home to the present moment and live in the light of mindfulness, concentration, and insight, you have no reason to worry about the future, and you have peace.

Success isn't a matter of talent alone. There are many elements that contribute to success. Even if you're the most talented person, even if you have real insight, if the right time has not come, you won't be successful. So you just do your best, and if conditions are sufficient you'll have success. You can never be sure that you'll be successful. That's the reality.

If you have a good manager, you have a better chance of being successful. Sometimes whether a book becomes a bestseller has nothing to do with the book. It depends on the way your publisher promotes the book. That is why I don't suffer when one of my books doesn't sell as well as another book. My desire is for my readers to get in touch with the Four Noble Truths of suffering and the way out of suffering. My goal is not fame, recognition, power, or money. I don't have a private bank account. I don't carry money. Whatever money my books earn goes to charitable causes and humanitarian projects such as helping hungry children in the Third World. So my concern is not money or fame. My concern is to satisfy my desire––my desire to serve, to help.

Many of the Buddha's teachings were not understood or appreciated during his lifetime. I have discovered that many of his teachings have not been explored and put into practice. Some have only begun to be understood in my generation. Yet the Buddha did not suffer because of this. He said, "Many of my teachings are difficult to believe." He was aware of this, but he had the courage to teach anyway.

The teaching of no-self is difficult to understand, and this was especially so during the lifetime of the Buddha. He lived in a society where nearly everyone believed in the self, the soul. But the Buddha had the courage to teach no-self, to go against the overwhelming majority in the religious and philosophical circles of India. Although few people followed his teaching at first, he was not unhappy, because he knew that if something is the truth, it will be the truth for a long time.

We can judge our success at work in many ways. Usually we judge it by how much money we make, what title we have, and

how much others recognize our achievements. But if you can
go to work each day as a bodhisattva, if your presence at work
brings you and others joy, then you have a successful work life.
You have succeeded in the present moment, the only moment
that exists.

EIGHT

Taking Care of
Nonbusiness

Business can't exist without nonbusiness elements. Your co-workers are part of your work environment, but they are also people, a nonbusiness element. The piece of paper you write on is made up of tree, sunshine, and water, as well as all the work that went into making it; these are some of the nonpaper elements of a sheet of paper. Seeing the nonbusiness elements in business is the teaching of interbeing. Nothing can exist by itself alone. Everything depends on everything else in order to be.

The Buddha said, "This is because that is." This means that nothing can exist by itself alone; things coexist with everything else. It also means that every phenomenon affects all other phenomena. The same is true with right and left. If right is there, left is there also. If we remove the right, the left cannot be there either. If we have a pencil and we try to cut off the right and leave only the left, the pencil will get shorter but we will still have a right and a left. It's like the flower and the garbage. We think the flower is not the garbage and the garbage is not the flower. But if we leave the flower for ten days, it becomes a piece of garbage. And if we know how to compost the garbage, in a few months it can become a flower. The flower and garbage inter-are.

The same is true for suffering and happiness. Because you know from your own experience what suffering is, you are able to identify happiness when it manifests. Therefore these two things are not really opposites or enemies; they engender each other. Suppose you're a conservative politician. You're likely to look at liberal politicians as your enemies. But the presence of the right wing makes the left wing possible. So you should wish for the left wing to exist for a long time, so that you can also exist.

If you're the head of a company, your practice is to do your work as head of the company. And the practice of the head of a company is to bring well-being into the company, not only for your employees but also for your suppliers and customers. Happiness is not an individual matter. Prosperity is not an individual matter. The well-being of our clients, our customers, our community, and our employees is linked together.

When you look deeply into a flower, you see that the flower cannot *be* by itself alone. When you look into the flower, you see the sunshine. If you remove the sunshine element, the flower cannot be there anymore. It will collapse, because the flower is sunshine. Sunshine is sunshine; it is not a flower. But sunshine is an element that makes up a flower. We call it a non-flower element. If you continue to look deeply into the flower, you will find other nonflower elements in it, like clouds. A cloud is a nonflower element, but without a cloud, the flower cannot be. If you try to take the element cloud from the flower, the flower will collapse. Earth and minerals are also nonflower elements. A flower is made of only nonflower elements. If you look deeply into the flower, you can't find any one element you can call flower. By taking care of nonflower elements, you take care of the flower.

In the same way, business is made of nonbusiness elements, and you need to take care of the nonbusiness elements for your business to do well. Your well-being, your capacity to smile, rest, and breathe, as well as your capacity to care for the well-being of your family, are nonbusiness elements, but they are essential to the well-being of business.

It's perfectly possible to work in business in the light of the teaching on interbeing. The well-being of the manager and the well-being of her family are crucial to the well-being of the company itself. And the well-being of the company is crucial to the well-being of the employees and their families. Everything is connected to everything else. When you take care of yourself, you take care of your family. When you behave responsibly toward your employees, it benefits your company.

Many people must spend most of their time working, away from their family, to stay competitive in their profession. It's a real challenge to balance family time with the pressures of a career. Yet you can conduct your business in such a way that it is not separate from the life of your family. Show interest in your family members' life outside the home. See their difficulties and successes as your own. You may offer support in a way that encourages everyone to find meaning and happiness in each other's work. When you see your partner's work as your own, you will no longer feel a separation between your family life and your work life. The physical absence during work time will not be a real absence.

Our family lives are important. Without our families, how can we know the warmth and tenderness of love, of being cared for and understood deeply? We should make our family into a sangha, a family of practice. The practice of mindfulness can also improve our life at home. When we indulge our habit energies of blaming and criticizing each other, we can lose our happiness or even our families. We can learn to practice loving speech and deep listening to bring more joy into our family. Even though we have lived with our family members for many years, we should not be too sure that we truly understand each other, that we know how to love each other. We need to learn how to really listen to each other, how to listen in such a way that we understand deeply each other's suffering. Only then can we know how to take care of and deeply love each other.

We can practice mindful eating together each day. We sit down for breakfast as a family and even if we have only fifteen minutes together, we can really be present for each other during those fifteen minutes. We really look at each other and we smile. We are aware how precious it is just to be together, and we don't waste that time. This is awareness; this is mindfulness; this is love.

The best way for us to share our practice with our families is through our way of living, not through our words. It is possible for us to drive our cars mindfully, enjoying breathing in and out, not letting ourselves be carried away by thinking about the past, the future, and our projects. And when we come to a red light, we smile to it as a friend, not as an enemy, because the red light says, "Stop! Go back to your breathing, and enjoy it." Before you open the door when you get home, you might pause and breathe in and out three times and smile, so that when your loved ones see you, you will be more pleasant after a hard day's work. When you make breakfast, you can transform breakfast making into a practice of love and happiness. Enjoy every moment of your breakfast making, and the kitchen will become a meditation hall. There is peace and calm, and you may invite your partner, your child, to join you. Then when you eat breakfast, eat in such a way that peace and freedom are possible. When you brush your teeth, can you take those one or two minutes to brush them in freedom and joy? And when you sit down and enjoy your tea or coffee after lunch, be peaceful, be free, and enjoy it deeply. Be fully present for your tea or coffee. It is possible for us to be grounded in the present moment and live each moment deeply with the energy of mindfulness and joy.

After several days of living like this, you will be calmer and more joyful, and your partner may ask, "Darling, how do you do it?" This is your chance to share your practice with him. Don't try to impose your practice on him. Just practice living deeply and mindfully, without any formalities. You don't need to show anyone that you are practicing. You walk in a natural way, but a mindful way. You eat naturally but mindfully. And your peace, your solidity, your joy will have an influence on the other person. If you have a friend or colleague who knows the practice, you may ask her to spend the weekend, or half a day, with you, because we need a community of practice supporting us.

You can also share your peace with colleagues in your workplace. During a meeting with your colleagues, your way of speaking, your way of listening, your way of smiling, your whole capacity to communicate will influence them. If we are skillful, we will succeed in bringing the practice to both our home and our workplace.

It is possible to make the workplace a place of practice. Our workplace is also a kind of family, a community, and we have to take care of our workplace so that we can profit from the energy of peace, stability, and freedom even during work time. There are those who have been able to bring the practice of mindfulness into their work life, using the practices of mindful walking, deep relaxation, and peaceful communication. While we walk from one meeting to the next, from one building to another, we can follow our breathing and be aware of each step we take. We can relax our bodies and mind and enjoy each moment without being caught in our worries and anxieties. This is mindfulness of walking; this is dwelling happily in the present moment. Then when we arrive at our destination we will be fresher and calmer.

A member of Congress wrote me that after attending a mindfulness retreat I offered for political representatives he has changed the way he walks at work. He always practices walking meditation, stopping his thinking completely. His office is busy: he has to answer many questions and deal with many matters. The only time when he can really stop his thinking and get a rest is when he walks from his office to the chamber to vote. He focuses his mind entirely on his breathing and his steps, not thinking at all. He said this helps him survive the hectic life of a congressman.

When we have a meeting with our colleagues, we can practice mindful speaking and listening, by staying in touch with our breathing and calming our mind. Our communication will be more successful because we are not caught by the energy of anger, confusion, or fear.

Some workplaces allow time each day for resting. They have found that setting aside periods of rest or deep relaxation actually increases productivity and effectiveness of work. When we can relax, we restore our well-being. We come back to ourselves and release all tensions and worries. There could be a special room in the workplace where employees can lie down for ten or twenty minutes. We can practice deep relaxation while sitting up. Many of my students in Europe and the United States have programmed their computers to imitate the sound of a bell every fifteen minutes, so that they can practice stopping. They hear the sound of the bell, and they let go of whatever they are doing for three or four in- and out-breaths. It is so simple; it is healing and nourishing to practice like that.

Mindfulness can improve the quality of our work life. Our work should be meaningful. This is important to our overall quality of life. We can work in such a way that we relieve suffering and benefit ourselves and others; or we can work in a way that increases our stress and suffering every day. Competition is there; running after more money, more fame, and more consumption is there; yet it is possible to stop. It is possible to look deeply at whether these things bring us true happiness. Are these things bringing us freedom from our pain and suffering? We must look into this matter: how can we bring more happiness, more peace, and more compassion into our work lives? We must take up this question with our colleagues and friends to discover concrete and specific steps we can take to change the situation. We need the support of a sangha, a group of friends who practice mindfulness. We need the support of wise friends who can offer us guidance and help us to get on the path of peace, happiness, and liberation.

You also have to care about the well-being of your customers. You cannot sell them just anything. You sell them only the things that will not harm their bodies or their consciousness. You know that right consumption, mindful consumption, is the only way out of the mess we have created in our society. We die as a result of wrong consumption. If you produce or sell things that destroy the bodies and consciousness of others, you destroy yourself and you destroy your company. Making money in this way is self-destruction. This is the insight of interbeing.

The same is true of our effect on the environment. It is possible for the element of love, of responsibility, to motivate us in our business. Having love as your motivation will not make your business less competitive. Rather it will make you more profitable, in addition to bringing you friendship and happiness. When we have love, we have the capacity to live according to the Five Mindfulness Trainings, including protecting life. If we think only about our income and we destroy the environment, we have no love and we harm other living beings. When we are aware that we are damaging the environment, this becomes a knot in our consciousness and we aren't at ease. Even though we earn good money, our uneasiness will grow until one day we will no longer be happy, we will not sleep well at night. Realizing this gives us the courage to change our livelihood so we can protect life. When we are motivated by love, we can easily avoid damaging others and destroying the environment.

Right livelihood is having a job that expresses your compassion and mindfulness. Even if your business brings in a lot of money, if it destroys the environment or other people, you must immediately say to yourself, "There is not enough love in my business, and I can't continue this way. I need to make changes so I can protect the environment, protect life." There are businesses that do this. A good example is Patagonia. (The story of this compassionate business is in Appendix B.) When we do business truly in a spirit of love, we never feel guilty, and we will not one day have to pay a high price for our guilt.

There is always a struggle inside us, but we must keep asking ourselves, what is our aim? Our aim is happiness, and love is the basic element of this happiness. When we have happiness, we do not have the heart to destroy the lives of other living beings. We must reexamine our idea of human superiority over other species and life forms. Humans are made of nonhuman elements. We appeared on the planet very late compared to other species. Protecting the lives of other species is protecting our own lives. Protecting nonhumans is protecting humans.

There are those who compete mercilessly, who don't respect any limits, who disregard business ethics; if we are not careful, we may think we have to follow them. But we can go another way, the way of love. In fact, love goes perfectly in tandem with success. Love can help us become even more successful than those whose motive is purely profit-driven. When we see people consumed by greed, we have compassion for them, because they pursue money and fame but aren't happy. We find skillful ways to help them. The best way is to show them by our example: we protect and love people and the environment, we are able to help others, and we are still successful. This will help them change. Only love helps us have a good relationship with other species, the environment, and planet Earth.

One day the Buddha was sitting in the woods with some of his monks. They had finished eating their lunch in silence, and they were about to start a dharma discussion, when a farmer came running up to them. The farmer looked unhappy: "Monks, have you seen my cows going by here?" The Buddha said, "No, we haven't seen any cows come by here." The farmer said, "Monks, I am a very unhappy person. I have only twelve cows, and I don't know why, but this morning they all ran away. And that's not all. I have twenty acres of sesame plants, and this year the insects have eaten everything. I think I'm going to die. How can I survive without my cows and my sesame seeds?" The Buddha looked at him with compassion and said, "Sorry, my friend, we haven't seen any cows passing this way. You might want to look for them in another direction." When the farmer had gone, the Buddha turned to his monks, looked at them deeply, smiled to them, and said, "Dear friends, do you know that you are lucky people? You don't have any cows to lose."

If you have a cow, you suffer because you are afraid of losing your cow. People in any profession have to learn not to make their work into a cow; this is a very important practice. You have to release your cows. You have to be free from your cows. The Buddha didn't have any cows, so he was never afraid of losing them. He was given the Bamboo Grove by King Bimbisara, as a place for him and his monks to stay. (You can visit the Bamboo Grove in India—it's still there.) When King Bimbisara presented this gift, he poured some water on the hands of the Buddha and declared, "My teacher, this Bamboo Grove is yours for you and your students to use." The Buddha kept silent as he accepted the gift.

But what if the next king wanted to take it back? The Buddha wouldn't suffer at all. He didn't need the Bamboo Grove to survive. He and his monks and nuns were happy to stay in other places, in a palm grove or a forest. All they needed each day was to be able to sit at the foot of a tree. The Buddha had the Bamboo Grove, but he didn't look on the Bamboo Grove as his cow. With or without that grove, he was the Buddha, free and happy.

In Plum Village, we live with several hundred people in four hamlets. There's the Upper Hamlet, the Lower Hamlet, the New Hamlet, and the Lower Mountain Hamlet. We practice not looking on the four hamlets as our cows. If for some reason we must close down one day, we'll be able to practice elsewhere and retain our happiness.

The practice of businesspeople, politicians, artists, teachers, parents, and all of us is to learn to look at our work as a noncow. You do your work in your company, in your organization, but you're free. You're not a slave of your job or any cow. You are simply working for the well-being of many people, including yourself.

In Zen circles, we like to tell the story of a man riding very fast on a horse. His friend standing at the side of the road hollers, "Where are you going?" The rider turns around and says, "I don't know, ask the horse!" The horse, not the man, is in control. The horse takes him wherever it wants. This is the situation for many of us. Our business is the horse, and the rider of the horse doesn't have any power to stop.

Many of us work as if we were on that horse. We need a work family to save us. When you commit to mindfulness, you're making an investment in yourself, and once you start investing in yourself, you'll begin to relieve the suffering of those around you and see their well-being as another good investment to make. To make this investment in others, you need to be a free person. If you are a slave to your business—your "busy-ness"—and to your ideas, you can't do it. You're intelligent enough to know that you have to devote time to yourself, your community, and your family, but as long as your work is holding the reins, you can't do it.

We all need friends, copractitioners, and teachers to be strong enough to practice. When three or four of you come together, you form a community. You become strong enough to create an atmosphere where you can resist the dictatorship of your business. Though your eyes may be bright, the eyes of one individual can't see as deeply or as far as the eyes of a community. We call them "sangha eyes." When we combine our intelligence, our concentration, and our wisdom, and we use sangha eyes to look into reality, we can discover much more than if we look only as an individual.

Many of us have a natural tendency to think of business wherever we are. Even when we are not officially at work, we may struggle with an urge to run and make a business phone call prompted by our worry. Much of our time is lost thinking and talking about our worries, even though we know very well that worrying doesn't improve things. The more we speak about them, the more worried we become. The more worried we become, the more we want to speak about them.

We are throwing away the time we've been given to live our life. Time is precious. There are people who say that time is money. But time is much more than money. Time is life. You are given twenty-four hours each day to live, not just to make money. That's why we have to organize a resistance to the momentum of running.

Without a sangha, without people who suffer from the same thing and are interested in changing it through mindfulness, we can't stop the horse. No matter how intelligent, how determined you are, you can't succeed in taming the horse by yourself. The habit energy is stronger than you. You need the sangha.

The person who works in the corporate world needs a community, a sangha, to put what they have learned, the dharma, into practice. Without others who are in the same situation supporting each other, the practice will be difficult if not impossible. Five, six, seven people who work in business and find themselves in the same situation with similar difficulties can come together and support each other to practice mindfulness.

When we are nourished in our family life and our work life, we will not have conflict. We will not feel pushed to do more, to compete, because we have already tasted true happiness and joy and we no longer have to run after anything. Being happy where we are is a deep practice. It depends a great deal on our way of seeing things, our way of using the time that we have together.

Most of us have a sense of responsibility about our work. But to focus on work is to focus on only one part of reality. This leaves us unable to respond to the total situation in the present moment. We need to have the capacity to respond to what is in the here and now. We need to learn how to be there for ourselves, our family, and the people we're responsible for in the business. We need reminders to help us stop our thinking and go back to breathing mindfully.

In Plum Village, when we hear a bell, we stop what we're doing, thinking, or saying, and we go back to our in-breath and our out-breath. "Breathing in, calming; breathing out, smiling." "Breathing in, I feel alive; breathing out, I smile to life." We breathe in and out at least three times. There are a lot of bells in Plum Village for us to practice with. Not only do we practice with an actual bell; whenever the telephone rings, it's an opportunity for us to go back to our in-breath and out-breath and stop thinking, talking, and moving. Imagine if you did this at work! Every time the cell phone or work phone rings, you could take a deep mindful breath before answering it. Even if your phone rings all the time, this wouldn't be a waste of time.

In Plum Village, we enjoy breathing in and out and smiling. This is already the practice of loving. We do the same when we hear the clock chiming every quarter hour. In the kitchen, the dining hall, wherever we hear these sounds, it's the voice of the Buddha within, calling us back to the here and now, inviting us to touch life deeply. In Plum Village this is easy to do because everyone is doing the same. It would be strange if you didn't do it. There is no one who is exempt. Each is expected to practice like everyone else. It is an opportunity to receive the support of the sangha, and in turn, each person's practice supports the practice of the sangha, the community of practitioners.

With your colleagues you could practice a "nonbusiness day." It doesn't mean this day is against business. This day can benefit every aspect of our life, including our business, but we don't let worries and fears interfere on this day. It should be free from worries and fear. This is something you can do by yourself, and it will strengthen your own mindfulness. Or a group of you can come together and organize a nonbusiness day when you devote yourselves to your well-being. This can be considered part of research and development. We have to look deeply to develop ways to increase our stability and happiness. This will be the basis for the well-being and stability of our company later on.

In the Judeo-Christian tradition, this is called a Sabbath day. In Buddhism, it's called the Uposatha day. Every monastic and every layperson in the Buddhist tradition observes the Uposatha day. On this day we recite the mindfulness trainings, we spend time together, and we enjoy each other's presence. In the time of the Buddha, people enjoyed four Uposatha days a month.

You don't have to have your whole staff on board. If four or five of you come together and practice living deeply each moment of the day, focusing on receiving the nourishment and healing you need, that will be a strong mindfulness practice. When four or five of you get together and practice mindful breathing and walking, embracing your difficulty and pain so as to transform it, this is a day of mindfulness. You can organize a day or a half-day of mindfulness to practice being there for yourself, your families, and your business.

If you have time, you can turn your "nonbusiness day" into a "nonbusiness retreat" that lasts a few days or a week. But even one day makes a huge difference. We call these one-day retreats or nonbusiness days, days of mindfulness. Many businesses have adopted them as quarterly or semiannual events. I know of a publishing company that goes hiking together at least four times a year. A movie production company that I know has a monthly event where they walk on the beach in sunny weather or go ice skating when it rains! Three or four of you can come together and plan a day of mindfulness. That is a day on which you train yourself to live deeply each moment of your life and not allow business to consume you. It's one day when you can be free from your worries and your tendency to dive into the future. It's only one day away from your work, but it will change the whole way you work.

Some suggestions for a nonbusiness day:

- A walk in the forest, on the beach, or in a park

- A weekend retreat in the mountains, with hiking and leisurely walks

- A tour of a factory unrelated to the work you do

- Horseback riding

- Whale watching, or going for a boat or ferry ride

- Surfing

- Snowshoeing or cross-country skiing

- Riding bicycles on a path or on quiet streets

- Table tennis, bowling, or pool

- A visit to a museum

- A picnic in the park

- A tour of a nature reserve or botanical garden

A nonbusiness day helps us honor the fact that each thing has its time. There is a time to eat. There is a time to water the garden. There is a time to discuss your work. So, when it's time to eat, you practice just eating and enjoying eating. You enjoy the present moment and eat with one hundred percent of yourself; otherwise you are not being kind to the food and the people sitting around the table. This is easy to understand. When you eat, just enjoy eating. Offer one hundred percent of yourself to the food and the people around you. This is the art of living, and it is very enjoyable.

When you spend time with a child, you need that time with the child and he or she needs that time with you. The time spent with this child should be devoted to only the child and yourself. No business, no future, and no past should be involved.

It takes training to master the art of living mindfully in the present moment. Everything has its own time—this is universal wisdom, not just Buddhist wisdom. You invest yourself one hundred percent in whatever you are doing in the moment. There are times when you have to discuss your work and business strategies. At that time, you invest one hundred percent of yourself into the practice of looking into the nature and difficulties of your business. If you are able to eat mindfully with concentration and spend time with your child mindfully with concentration, then, when the time for doing business comes, you will be able to look deeply into matters at hand and that time will be productive.

I'm a writer. I write stories, essays, books, and poems. There are times when I don't write. But that doesn't mean that writing isn't continuing inside me. When I water the vegetables, I just practice watering the vegetables. I enjoy watering my vegetable garden. I don't think about the poem or the short story, but I know that somewhere inside me the short story is being made. If I don't grow the lettuce, I can't write poems.

So when you grow lettuce, you have to grow it with one hundred percent of yourself and enjoy deeply the work of growing lettuce. Then, when you write a poem, the poem will be good. The moment you begin to write the words down is not exactly the moment you create the poem. While you practice mindful walking, breathing, and planting lettuce, without thinking at all about the poem, the poem is being written. The poem, or any work of art, is conceived in the depth of your consciousness while you're not thinking about it. The moment you write it down or express it is only the moment of completion, like when a mother gives birth to her baby. Much has happened before this to make the baby or the artwork possible. This is why there must be moments when you allow the child in you to grow. The same is true with your business and your plans for the future. If you do well what you are doing in the here and now, then when the time comes for you to do other things you will do them well, with great concentration and insight.

Learning to appreciate times of silence and nonaction are crucial for our productivity and this blossoming of concentration and insight. A businessman once told me, "When there's silence during a conversation, I feel uneasy and I want to say something to break the silence. What can I do?" In Plum Village silence is precious. We call it Noble Silence, and we

cherish it. It's more precious than gold. Silence can be eloquent. You sit there and your personality just shines, you radiate peace and joy. This is nonaction. You need only sit there,
and children like to come and sit close to you. Silence is very
important. It allows, it helps life to be. We have to retrain ourselves to enjoy silence.

Two friends sitting and having a cup of tea together may
spend half an hour in silence, yet they don't feel a void. When
I spent a winter at Princeton University, I used to visit an old
man who lived near the campus. His name was Luther Pfahler
Eisenhart. He was a mathematician, a friend of Albert Einstein's.
Every time I came, which was usually at night, he would open
the door for me and take me in close to the fireplace. Then his
wife would offer me a cup of tea and we would spend an hour
just sitting there—he didn't say anything and I didn't say anything. After that, I'd bow to him and go home.

That happened many times. I knew in advance that whenever I came, the same thing would happen. Yet I always came,
because it was very nice and very rewarding. We need to learn
again how to be silent. This is what the Buddha teaches us. Silence can be more intimate than talking. It is a way of being
that makes your doing, your action, deeper and more effective.

Walking from our room to the meditation hall, we walk in
such a way that each step brings us peace and joy. Walking like
that is being. Drinking our tea in freedom—this is the art of
being. Looking at another person in such a way that our understanding and compassion can be expressed—this is nonaction,

and it is already happiness. We make people happy by the way we live our daily lives.

When we become novice monks or nuns, our practice is to be happy novices. We don't need to be fully ordained monks or nuns to be happy. If we think like that, we sacrifice our novice lives. In fact, when we are novices, we have less to do and we can enjoy more. When you are a big brother, you have to take care of so many things! It is the same when you are a student— you don't need a diploma to be happy. If you are a lower-level manager in your company, you don't need to be the CEO to be happy. To feel happy right where you are in the present moment is your practice. With this kind of understanding, you accept yourself completely; you don't feel the need to become someone because you are already someone.

I remember one day I was having tea with a novice monk, and I said, "My child, do you want me to become a Buddha quickly?" And guess what he said: "No, I want you to be like this. That's good enough for me!"

I take my time. I want to be myself. I don't deny myself in the here and now. This is our practice—we call it aimlessness. We don't put a goal in front of ourselves and run after it constantly. If we do, we'll be running all our life and never be happy. Happiness is possible only when you stop running and cherish the present moment and who you are. Who you are is already a wonder; you don't need to be someone else. You are a wonder of life.

NINE

Sparking a Collective Awakening

Even if you cultivate the five powers of faith, diligence, mindfulness, concentration, and insight, if you think you can cultivate them for yourself alone, your power will remain weak. The insight of interbeing teaches us that only when we acknowledge and awaken our collective consciousness can we harness the full strength of our collective power.

There is individual consciousness, and there is collective consciousness. Our consciousness is composed of all the seeds sown by our past actions and the past actions of our family and society. Every day our thoughts, words, and actions flow into the sea of our consciousness and create our bodies, minds, and the world. The individual consciousness is made of the collective, and the collective is made of the individual; they inter-are. Your idea of beauty doesn't come only from within you. You think something is beautiful because many people consider it beautiful. You're influenced by the collective consciousness. Like fashion: you desire a certain style of clothing based on what others decide is fashionable. If the majority considers it to be beautiful, you agree that it is beautiful. You may go to an art exhibit and see a number of paintings that you don't find beautiful at all. But all the people who come to the exhibit praise and appreciate these paintings, so you pretend that they are beautiful also. You try to look at them in such a way that you also see them as beautiful. And later on, because of the collective consciousness, you see them as beautiful. Beauty and ugliness, like many of our values, are creations of our collective consciousness.

When fear becomes collective, when anger becomes collective, it is extremely dangerous. It is overwhelming. This is why you have to choose an environment where you'll be influenced by a healthy, clear collective consciousness. We are easily influenced by collective thinking. In 2004, eighty percent of the American population still believed the war in Iraq was a response to the attacks of September 11, 2001, even though there was no link between the Iraqi government and Al Qaeda. In September 2004, only thirty-five percent of the English population thought the war was correct. Citizens of the United States have to be open to the perspective of the Indians, the Asians, the Africans, the Arabs, and the Latin Americans. You have to listen to them; you have to understand how they think and how they understand situations. You cannot lock yourself in one notion, one idea. The mass media and the military-industrial complex create a prison for us, so we continue to think, see, and act in the same way. It is up to each of us, individually and collectively, to free ourselves from this prison of views, of fear and violence.

As an artist, teacher, politician, or businessperson, you can influence people and create beauty. You should have your own insight. You can help the good, the true, and the beautiful already there inside you to manifest. You express yourself in the light of truth. Even if the majority has not seen the truth that you have, you are courageous enough to continue. And the minority who see the truth, who are awakened, can transform the whole situation. Just as our individual consciousness is created and influenced by the collective, our individual consciousness can influence and create the collective consciousness.

We may be clear about the need for change in our country, but we need the courage to express ourselves even when the majority is going in the opposite direction. We should be supported by our loved ones, by our colleagues who agree with us—because a change of direction can happen only when there is a collective awakening. Individuals and small groups can spark a change in consciousness. Even if we are a minority, if we believe we have an insight that can lead us out of our difficult situation, we should have the courage to speak out. There are many ways in which we can succeed in speaking out—and not just as an individual, because there may be a number of us who think clearly but haven't had the opportunity to show our light. Therefore it is very important to say "I am here!" to those who share the same kind of insight. Please raise your voice so that you can come together with others. When we come together, we can voice our concerns strongly and effectively. Because collective awakening is the only thing that can change our situation.

During the war in Vietnam, I was almost shot by an American army officer because he thought I was a guerrilla in disguise. Before American soldiers came to Vietnam, they were told that anyone could be a communist guerrilla, including Buddhist monks. I remained calm and was able to ease his fear. My sangha and I practiced seeing the suffering not only of the communist and anticommunist factions, but also of the American soldiers, sent so far from home to kill or be killed. I was free from hatred because I had understanding and compassion, and many of us survived the war thanks to this practice.

My experience with several wars in Vietnam has led me to the firm belief that terrorism cannot be removed by force and that deep listening is more powerful than bombs. Terrorism is born from wrong perceptions. The terrorists have wrong perceptions of themselves. They have wrong perceptions of us. That is why they want to destroy us, to punish us. If we know how they think, how they perceive things, we can help them remove these wrong perceptions. The work of removing wrong perceptions is the foundation for transforming violence and terrorism and fostering peace.

We have to listen to other political leaders in Europe, in Asia, because our feeling, our thinking, may be characterized by a lot of wrong perceptions. We should not be too sure of our perceptions. Our wrong perceptions lead to conflict, suffering, and war. Americans now are a bit lonely in their way of seeing things, and they need to listen to Asians, Europeans, Africans, everyone. When you are able to remove your wrong perceptions and help remove the wrong perceptions in others, then you remove terrorism. There is no other way. It is clear that the war on terrorism has not helped reduce terrorism. It has created much more hatred and fear both inside and outside the United States. America is more vulnerable now than in 2001. The war on terrorism has forced us to look at each other as potential terrorists. When you travel by plane, you are searched. They are not looking for your Buddha nature; they are looking for your terrorist nature.

Everyone can participate in the work of awakening, helping enlightenment to be born in society. Awakening is your task. By skillful means, you can contribute greatly to the collective awakening that is the foundation of all change. You can help people see that deep, compassionate listening and loving speech are the only ways to remove wrong perceptions.

Unfortunately, our politicians are not used to this kind of practice, and the collective idea is that money and military power are the only kinds of power we have. But we do have other kinds of power. America has the power of understanding and the power of compassion, if we choose to use them. There are more than enough people in America who have insight, understanding, and compassion. If they come together to voice their concern and offer us the light, we can overcome this difficult moment. The path is the path of peace. It is my conviction that there is no way to peace—peace *is* the way. You have to use peaceful means to arrive at peace.

The United States cannot do everything in the world. Although she is the mightiest nation, the United States is only one member of the community of all nations. She has to allow other nations to be responsible for the world, and not try to do everything by herself. The United States needs to invest in the

United Nations and allow other countries to participate in building the United Nations into a real organization for peace, with sufficient authority and power.

If we consider violence to be a disease, we can use the medicine of deep listening to treat it. I don't think we can heal the disease of violence in our families and our schools using money alone. If legislators look deeply into this matter, they will see that high levels of violence at home have to do with our foreign policy. When there is violence inside us, it is easy to commit or condone violence against another person; when there is war in ourselves, it is easy to start a war with another person. Couples, families, and nations are the same.

Why don't we create a law that gives parents a chance to go to a workshop, a retreat, every year—seven days to learn how to take care of each other, to restore communication, mutual understanding, and love? Why don't we allow schoolteachers to go on a paid retreat each year so they can learn how to transform their suffering and understand the suffering of their students?

Once we have engaged in this kind of peace education, we can help our children cultivate the five spiritual powers. If you are a schoolteacher or a parent, you can teach your children or students to cultivate the five spiritual powers. Please begin now, and soon we will have a new generation of people who know what kind of power they really need to be truly happy. We should organize mindfulness retreats for parents and schoolteachers and ask them to initiate this education for future generations.

In Thailand and other Buddhist countries, in the old times

young men were supposed to spend one year in a temple to receive spiritual training. They had mandatory spiritual service instead of military service. Even the prince had to spend one year in a monastery before becoming king. This was a beautiful thing! But now the time has been reduced to a month or a few weeks, which is not long enough. It is my dream to set up a peace institute where young people can be trained before they marry in concrete methods of creating happiness and peace in the family. If you are a happy couple, the children you raise will also be happy.

If we ourselves haven't cultivated these spiritual powers, we cannot help our children or others to do it. We have to cross the river of suffering in order to help other people across. We have to become enlightened so as to help other people become enlightened. Most of us in the world are still living in a dream, and we don't know what we are doing. We are taking each other in the direction of destruction, but we don't know it. Enlightenment is crucial to our survival.

Many of us believe that we are powerless, that we can't do much to change the situations around us, especially political situations. The reality is that we can always be someone and do something to help change the situation. Like us, our political leaders have positive seeds and negative seeds. They may be surrounded by people who don't water the good seeds in them. Their advisors continue to water the seeds of fear, craving, anger, and violence in them. We have to find ways to get in touch with our political leaders and help them. Protesting is a kind of help, but it should be done skillfully, so people see it as an act of love and not an attack.

The fact is that the majority of us are so busy with our small, daily problems that we are indifferent. Maybe we care, but we are so busy with our small sufferings, our small miseries that we don't have the time and energy to do these important things. But it really doesn't take a lot of time. We can write a love letter to our political representatives. This is a little more challenging than writing a letter of protest. Here is an example of such a love letter that I wrote to the president of the United States.

Dear Mr. President,

Last night, I saw my brother (who died two weeks ago in the United States) come back to me in a dream. He was with his children. He told me, "Let's go home together." After a millisecond of hesitation, I told him joyfully, "Okay, let's go."

Waking up from that dream at five this morning, I thought of the situation in the Middle East, and for the first time, I was able to cry. I cried for a long time, and I felt much better after about one hour. Then I went to the kitchen and made some tea. While making tea, I realized that what my brother had said is true: our home is large enough for all of us. Let us go home as brothers and sisters.

Mr. President, I think that if you can allow yourself to cry like I did this morning, you will also feel much better. It is our brothers that we kill over there. They are our brothers—God tells us so, and we also know it. They may not see us as brothers because of their anger, their misunderstanding, and their discrimination. But with some awakening, we can see things in a different way, and this will allow us to respond differently to the situation. I trust God in you; I trust the Buddha nature in you.

Thank you for reading.

> In gratitude and with brotherhood,
> Thich Nhat Hanh
> Plum Village

Honorable George W. Bush
The White House
Washington D.C., U.S.A.

Plum Village
Le Pey 24240 Thénac
France

8.8.06

Dear Mr. President,

Last night, i saw my brother (who died two weeks ago in the U.S.A.) coming back to me in a dream. He was with all his children. He told me, "Let's go home together." After a millisecond of hesitation, i told him joyfully, "OK; let's go."

Waking up from that dream at 5am this morning, i thought of the situation in the Middle East; and for the first time, i was able to cry. I cried for a long time, and i felt much better after about one hour. Then i went to the kitchen and made some tea. While making tea, i realized that what my brother had said is true: our home is large enough for all of us. Let us go home as brothers and sisters.

Mr. President, i think that if you could allow yourself to cry like i did this morning, you will also feel much better. It is our brothers that we kill over there. They are our brothers, God tells us so, and we also know it. They may not see us as brothers because of their anger, their misunderstanding, their discrimination. But with some awakening, we can see things in a different way, and this will allow us to respond differently to the situation. I trust God in you, i trust the Buddha nature in you. Thank you for reading.

In gratitude and
with brotherhood

Thich Nhat Hanh
Plum Village

By living your life mindfully, by expressing your creativity and wisdom in your work, you can contribute to a collective awakening of our people. Then we'll be strong enough to influence our political leaders. We have to support our leaders. We have to help them see the situation more clearly: that their present course of action is causing a lot of destruction and damage, that the war on terrorism has created more hate, more terror, and more terrorists. We can show people that violence is not working. Only with compassionate listening and gentle speech can you help remove the wrong perceptions that are at the foundation of hate and violence.

We need to manage our feelings of powerlessness, of being overwhelmed by despair. We do have power, and we should know how to use it to effect change. We have to organize ourselves. Openness and loving speech can work miracles. Every parent, teacher, businessperson, and artist can always do something to encourage collective awakening. Everyone is responsible. The situation is too important to leave to politicians alone. Without collective awakening, nothing will happen. Awakening is the foundation of every kind of change. Each of us has to sit down and look deeply to see what we can be and what we can do today.

In September 2006, I was invited to speak at the United Nations Educational, Scientific and Cultural Organization (UNESCO). I proposed that UNESCO organize regular "no-car days" all over the globe as a wonderful way to educate people about what is happening to our environment. In all the Plum Village practice centers in North America, Europe, and Vietnam, we have begun to practice one no-car day a week.

We arrange things in advance so on that day none of us will have to drive anywhere. Already many, many people around the world have committed themselves to doing the same. Our goal is to reduce our driving by fifty percent. We have begun to use cars that run on vegetable oil and do not increase carbon dioxide levels in the atmosphere, as well as organizing regular no-electricity days. We will also participate in and encourage others to join the World Car Free Day on September 22 every year (to learn more and get involved, visit our Web site www.car-free-days.org and www.worldcarfree.net/wcfd). Talking about the danger is not enough. We have to do something and invite other people to join in.

People sometimes ask me how our species can reconcile with planet Earth after all the harm we have caused. We can reconcile with Mother Earth by practicing walking meditation. On every step we can kiss the earth with our feet, with love, with the promise that we will stop our current course of destroying Mother Earth. If we continue abusing the earth this way, there is no doubt that our civilization will be destroyed. This turnaround takes enlightenment, awakening. The Buddha attained individual awakening. Now we need a collective enlightenment to stop this course of destruction. Civilization is going to end if we continue to drown in the competition for power, fame, sex, and profit.

One day during meditation, I was contemplating global warming, the tsunami in Southeast Asia, weather changes, and so on. With some anguish, I asked Nature this question: "Nature, do you think we can rely on you?" I asked the question because I know that Nature is intelligent; she knows how to react, sometimes violently, to reestablish balance. And I heard the answer in the form of another question: "Can *I* rely on *you?*" The question was being put back to me: can Nature rely on humans? And after long, deep breathing, I said, "Yes, you can mostly rely on me." And then I heard Nature's answer, "Yes, you can also mostly rely on me." That was a very deep conversation I had with Nature.

This should not be a mere verbal declaration. It should be a deep commitment from everyone, so that nature can respond in kind. With collective insight we can reconcile with and heal our planet. Each of us can do something in our own daily lives to contribute, to ensure that a future is possible for the next generation.

Recently, I had the experience of seeing the power of a collective awakening when I returned to Vietnam with a large sangha after nearly forty years in exile. I came to the West at the age of forty. It was 1966, and I went to the United States to call for a cessation of the bombing. The United States had half a million soldiers in Vietnam. At the end of the war, more than fifty thousand of them had been killed or lost. Many millions of Vietnamese civilians died during the war. The land, forests, and water were polluted, destroyed by chemical poisons. By that time, I was already a well-known teacher and writer in my country. I intended to stay in the United States for three months, to tour the country and speak about the need to stop the fighting. But after three months, I learned that the government of Vietnam didn't want me to go home because I had dared to call for peace.

Many of us in Vietnam had suffered so much, and we had seen so much suffering around us caused by the war, that we had to speak out. We were caught between two warring parties and we had to speak out. But many of us had no means to express ourselves. We had no radio, no television, and no newspaper that would cover the truth of our situation. Those who dared to speak out against the war were arrested. So some people immolated themselves to attract attention to the plight of the masses of Vietnamese who didn't want war. Only then did the press begin to realize that the majority of Vietnamese people didn't accept the war. That is why I decided to travel to the West—to tell the world about the suffering of the Vietnamese nation and people.

After I learned that the government of South Vietnam didn't want me to go home, I continued my appeals in America for peace, and then I went to Europe, Asia, and Australia. Finally I settled in Paris and set up a community of practice to continue the work of calling for peace.

During nearly forty years in exile, we made attempts to negotiate my return to Vietnam. Finally, in January 2005, I was able to go home. When I first left Vietnam, I was like a cell removed from its body. The sangha is like a body, and each member is just a cell of the body. But I didn't dry up and die as a cell, because I brought the whole sangha in my heart. I went to the West for my sangha and not as an individual, and right away I began to build a little sangha in the West. Now, after forty years, my sangha in the West is not so small.

I wanted to go home to Vietnam as a sangha, not as a cell. Ultimately, two hundred people traveled with us back to Vietnam. We wanted to come as a true sangha, to show our practice of understanding and love, because we knew that if our practice was solid, strong, and authentic, we would be able to transform the fear and suspicion of the government.

The members of our delegation practiced well. At the hotel, the laypersons practiced sitting meditation in the morning. They ate only vegetarian food, they never touched alcohol, they were silent, and they lived together as a sangha, in harmony, in brotherhood and sisterhood. The hotel managers were impressed and said, "They have transformed our hotel into a meditation hall."

The trip was difficult because there was so much fear, so much suspicion. The Museum of War Criminals in Saigon had been displaying my picture and the picture of Sister Chan Khong, my assistant during the last fifty years. Before I arrived, because of some protest, my picture was removed. But the picture of Sister Chan Khong was still exhibited there during our three-month trip.

In addition, during my nearly forty years of exile, my books had been banned in Vietnam by both the communist and anticommunist regimes, because my books promoted peace and brotherhood, which both governments considered dangerous. We had negotiated an agreement that twelve of my books would be published before my arrival. But when we got to Vietnam, only four had been published. The fear was so great!

It took the whole of our three-month trip for the Vietnamese government to open up to us. The presence of the sangha of nuns, monks, laywomen, and laymen helped tremendously. The people saw Westerners learning meditation and practicing well. This inspired them. During the talks, we witnessed the transformation right before our eyes. We were able to remove a lot of wrong perceptions in people. Now they know much better who we are, because much fear and suspicion has been removed. If we had not been able to support each other using the power of the sangha, and to call on the seeds of patience, understanding, and compassion in ourselves, we would have reacted angrily and left the country halfway through the trip.

In the beginning of our trip, it was clear that the government didn't want us to teach, to be in touch with the people. We knew that our practice had to be stable and solid to succeed. The conservative wing of the government tried everything to prevent people from attending my lectures and being exposed to our presence. Before we arrived, we learned that many monks and nuns had been warned that they should not attend events with our sangha or they would be in trouble after we left.

Yet we continued to be humble and calm, and to smile. Finally there was a breakthrough. The Institute of Political Science in Saigon allowed us to organize a talk for intellectuals, scholars, Communist Party members, and government officials. They provided seats for three hundred people. But because we were practicing loving speech and deep listening, at the last minute we were able to persuade them to let the crowd come in. On that day more than one thousand attended the talk. I shared our experience of teaching the practice in the West. They were very interested. At the end they asked a number of questions, among them this one: "If you take refuge in the Three Jewels (the Buddha, the dharma, and the sangha) do you still have the right to love your country and the Communist Party?" My answer came very quickly and was very simple: "If taking refuge in the Three Jewels means you lose your right to love your country and the party, what is the use of taking the Refuges?" Everyone applauded for a long time. This sentence was reported to the central government and every arm of the party.

This is why, when we went to Hue, we were allowed to give a talk for Communist Party members, intellectuals, and government officials. Six or seven thousand people came. And when we went to Hanoi for the second time, five talks were organized for Communist Party members, government officials, and scholars. It turned out all of them were hungry for spirituality. Being with our delegation and me was an opportunity for them to express this openly. At the Political Institute of Ho Chi Minh in Hanoi, several organizers commented that dialogue and discussion between Marxism and Buddhism is crucial. They acknowledged that they could learn a lot from Buddhism. And a Communist Party member even dared to say that the party had made mistakes. Organizers expressed a desire to renew their country and learn more. The atmosphere was open and human. And you could feel the freedom. You could touch freedom of speech. It was wonderful: it may have been the first time people dared to speak out like that.

I was able to be direct, but I did not hurt anyone because my heart was full of compassion and brotherhood. I said things like, "You know, in Plum Village we live simply. Monks, nuns, and laypersons—we live together like a family. No one has a private car. No one has a private bank account. No one has a private telephone. Actually, we are the true communists." They laughed and laughed. They were not angry at all. And our message got through.

There were people who feared for my safety because I dared to address important issues, including corruption in the government. Yet we felt we could tell the truth; we could share what was in our heart, because we knew how to use the language of loving speech. As a result of this attention to using skillful means to reach people, the level of fear and anger went down every day, and a real change of heart took place in the government. This experience showed us powerfully how a small minority practicing diligently can influence the majority. The individual can indeed transform the collective.

You have just this one moment, and you can make a choice. You can chase your cravings, and perhaps to the outside world you will look powerful, but I can guarantee you will not find happiness. Or you can cultivate the five spiritual powers and bring to yourself, your loved ones, your work environment, and your community the power of the bodhisattva. It is this path that can bring you real happiness. It is the only path that can transform the world.

APPENDIX A

Meditations to Cultivate Power

Here are a number of concrete practices that strengthen our power, our spiritual energy, and that can be applied, or let us say *enjoyed*, anywhere at any time. Many of these practices can be considered kinds of meditation. When you think of meditation, you may think of a monk sitting absolutely still, undisturbed by sound or interruption. That is one kind of meditation, but there are many others you can enjoy at home or at work in just a few minutes.

Meditation consists of two elements. The first element is stopping, calming the mind, and concentrating. The second is looking deeply to get insight. In the first, you focus your mind on just one thing, like your steps or your breath. Concentration always means concentrating on something. Mindfulness is always mindfulness of something. You cannot concentrate on or become mindful of nothing. So to practice mindfulness you need an object. When you focus your attention on your breath, your breathing is the object of your mindfulness and concentration. When you generate the energy of mindfulness, it will embrace the object of your attention and keep it alive in your mind.

If you continue your concentration, you will be able to attain some insight, the second step of meditation. For instance, when you experience irritation or anger, you might focus your attention on it to find its root cause. Then, if you practice mindfulness and concentration for some time, you'll get to know the real nature of your anger, and your insight will liberate you from it. When the object of your inquiry is interesting, mindfulness and concentration are easy. When a talk or presentation is interesting, it's much easier for you to pay attention. If it is boring, you can do your best but it will be difficult to concentrate fully. Therefore, one key to success is to select an object of mindfulness and concentration that is interesting to you. If it is interesting, you'll get insight quickly.

MINDFUL BREATHING

There is a short poem I suggest you memorize to help you in the practice of mindful breathing. Whether you are practicing mindful sitting or walking, you may use this poem:

In, out
Deep, slow
Calm, ease

Smile, release
Present moment, wonderful moment.

The first two words, "In, out," mean, "Breathing in, I know I'm breathing in; breathing out, I know I'm breathing out." When you breathe in, you concentrate on only one thing, your in-breath. You take your mind off everything else and focus entirely on your in-breath. In the same way, you then concentrate on your out-breath. This is the first exercise. You can continue to silently repeat the words "In, out" to help you stay with the whole of your in-breath and your out-breath.

Don't take your mind off your breath and allow it to go somewhere else: "Breathing in, I know . . . oh, I forgot to turn the light off in my room." This is not concentration, because your mind is jumping from one thing to another. Practice staying with your in-breath from its beginning to its end. Your in-breath may last only four or five seconds. Everyone is capable of being one hundred percent with his in-breath for this length of time. When you practice mindfully breathing in and out for one minute, you stop your thinking for one minute. It's wonderful to stop your thinking and just *be*. Most of our thinking is an obstacle to being, because when you're absorbed in thinking, you aren't present and fully alive and you can't touch the wonders of life. "I think, therefore I am *not!*" "I think therefore I get lost in my thinking." To get lost in thinking is not to be.

Suppose your son or daughter is with you, smiling and beautiful as a flower. If you are busy thinking of the past, the future, your projects, your difficulties, and your sorrow, you are lost in your thinking. Then your beautiful little boy or girl is not available to you because you are not there. You are lost in your thinking. Not getting carried away by your thinking, then, means to be in the here and now, in order to encounter the wonders of life that are available: your little boy or your little girl. It means that you are available to them, and they are available to you.

Just one in-breath and one out-breath can help you stop your habitual thinking and go back to the here and now. When you go back to mindful breathing, your mind will connect right away with your body. In your daily life, your body may be there but your mind is elsewhere. Fortunately we have our breath, which serves as a bridge between them. The moment you go back to your breathing and breathe mindfully, your mind and your body come back together. It's wonderful, and it's very easy. It doesn't take a lot of time—maybe five or ten seconds at the most—and suddenly from a state of dispersion, you become mindful, you become concentrated. Because your mind has come back to your body, you have become truly present. You are really there, and when you are there, something else will be there also: life, as well as your beloved.

Even when you drive your car, you may concentrate on breathing in and out in order to be truly present. It's safer to drive when you are really there and not lost in your worries and anxiety. When you water the flowers in your front yard, practice mindful breathing to be fully present and enjoy the flowers and the act of watering. Then, once you know how to practice mindful breathing when you drive, wash dishes, or walk from one building to another, you can invite members of your family to do so too. You can sit together in your living room and practice breathing mindfully together. You don't need to watch television. The whole family can sit and really enjoy each other's presence, and a feeling of unity and peace will arise. It's a wonderful practice. Why not share the practice of mindful breathing with your co-workers too? You can teach them how to take care of their fatigue, their strong emotions, and their suffering.

You might like to stop reading this page now to practice "In, out" for one, two, or three minutes until you are really focused on your in-breath and out-breath. You'll realize that the quality of your breathing improves quickly. Don't try to make anything happen. All by itself, your in-breath becomes deeper and your out-breath becomes slower, more relaxed, soothing.

SITTING MEDITATION

To sit is a privilege. When Nelson Mandela visited France for the first time after he was released from prison, the press interviewed him and asked what he wanted to do the most. He answered, "Sit down and do nothing. Since the time of my release from prison, I haven't had that luxury. I've been so busy. So the thing I wish for the most is to sit down and do nothing." To have the opportunity to sit down and enjoy your in-breath and out-breath is already a wonderful thing. Breathing in and breathing out, you don't have to struggle. Please do it for Nelson Mandela; do it for all the people who are running and don't have time to return to themselves and just be. In our time, it's a luxury to just sit and not do anything. It's also crucial to our healing and nourishment.

Find a comfortable position either on a cushion or a chair. If you sit in a chair, rest both feet flat on the floor. Sit with your back straight, but not rigid. Release the weight of your body on to the cushion or chair, let your belly soften. Bring all your attention to your in and out breath. When your mind wanders, because it will, just gently bring your awareness back to your breath.

Sitting meditation is first of all just doing nothing and allowing yourself to relax. If you know the art of breathing and smiling, the pleasure of sitting will grow greater and greater. Then, with mindfulness and concentration, you can begin to see more deeply into the reality of your body, the reality of your consciousness, and the reality of your situation. When you see clearly, you're not likely to make so many mistakes. You have a chance to do the right thing in order to bring well-being to yourself and the people you love. That's the benefit of sitting.

MINDFUL WALKING

I want to say a bit more about the practice of mindful walking that I introduced in chapter 3. Everyone needs to walk. When we walk from work to the subway, the parking lot, or the restroom, whether we are going several blocks or just a few steps, we can always enjoy walking meditation. It means we learn to walk with awareness of every step we take, free of thinking and free of our projects.

If you want to walk peacefully, you may take two or three steps during your in-breath. When I breathe in, I usually take two steps and say, "In, in." I say it with my feet. I don't say it aloud with my mouth. I focus my attention on the soles of my feet. I touch the ground as if I am kissing the earth with my feet, with a lot of love. When I breathe out, I take two more steps and say, "Out, out." So the rhythm is "In, in. Out, out." Touch the earth mindfully. Let your breathing be natural, and coordinate your steps with your breathing. Don't stay in your head, but bring your attention down to the soles of your feet. You'll notice that your steps will be much more solid, much more stable. That stability will come into your body and your consciousness. Walk like a free person. You are no longer a slave of your projects, of your worries. Every step you take helps you reclaim your freedom.

I walk because I want to walk, not because someone pushes me or forces me to walk. I walk as a free person, and I enjoy every step I take. I don't rush, because I want to really be in the here and now and to touch life with every step I take. "In, in. Out, out." It can be very pleasant because you feel that freedom inside you. *You* are the one who is walking; you aren't being pulled by the past, the future, or your projects. You are yourself, you are the boss.

After practicing the first exercise of the poem, you continue with "Deep, slow." "Deep, deep. Slow, slow." You can say "deep" with each step you take on an in-breath, and "slow" with each step you take on an out-breath. Say it with your feet, not with your mind. You are aware of the number of steps your lungs want you to take during your in-breath and your out-breath, whatever is pleasant for you. If you experience walking as hard work, you aren't practicing correctly. The practice should be healing, transforming, and pleasant at the same time.

Next you might choose "Calm, ease." Don't say the words mechanically. When you say the word *calm* with your feet, you must feel the calm in your body or feelings. When you are concentrated and enjoy your steps, you support all of us who are trying to do the same thing. And when you practice mindful walking with others, you are also supported by their presence and their practice, and if you enjoy every step you take with solidity and freedom, with calm and ease, you contribute much to the quality of everyone's life.

You have to be able to release, to let go. Whatever has happened, this problem or that event, should not cause you to lose your happiness and peace, because you have the Buddha, the energy of awakening, within you. The Buddha is with you when you smile mindfully. The Buddha is with you when you walk mindfully. The Buddha is with you when you drink tea peacefully. You know you're capable of drinking your tea that way. You're capable of walking that way, and you're capable of breathing that way. Don't think that the Buddha is abstract. The Buddha is very concrete. The Buddha is the energy of mindfulness that is always available to you, if you know how to use it.

I know a businesswoman who always practices mindful walking from one building to another. Instead of running, she allows herself enough time to enjoy every step she takes. And during that time, she really stops thinking about business. She knows how to treat herself with love.

Walking mindfully is something all of us can learn. It's wonderful to feel that we're alive, walking on this beautiful planet. Many of us are used to running, and we're not capable of living deeply in the here and now. If we walk only to arrive somewhere else, we sacrifice the walking itself. Then there's no life during the time of walking. That is a loss. Where is the Kingdom of God? The Kingdom of God is available in the here and now. If you know how to walk mindfully, you can touch the Kingdom of God with every step you take. It's a matter of training only. There are so many wonders of life available to us right now.

One day in the Lower Hamlet we practiced walking meditation with many Catholic nuns and monks. I led the walk. We went through a meadow on the way to the woods. It was springtime and there were many tiny flowers of different colors in the grass. Because we walked mindfully and enjoyed every step we took, we got in touch with the wonders of life that were available in the month of May. The walk was joyful and healing. No one said anything. We just enjoyed touching the earth with our feet and connecting with whatever was present in the here and now. When we arrived in the woods, we sat down, listened to the birds, and enjoyed the sunshine filtering through the leaves. It was beautiful. We were able to touch the miracle of life that was present. Most of us were monks and nuns, Buddhist and Catholic. I turned to a French monk from Plum Village, and I said, "Brother, paradise is now or never." I said it in French, *"Le paradis est maintenant ou jamais,"* and he nodded and smiled. Paradise is not an idea. The Kingdom of

God is not an idea. It's a reality, because life is right here with all its wonders.

If we're not capable of being in the here and now, we're not capable of entering into the Kingdom of God, or into paradise. But with some training, we will be able to stop in the here and now and touch life deeply. Then everything else in our life will improve, because we will have more solidity, more freedom, and more happiness. Taking time to walk regularly in this way will help us transform ourselves, so that we can take better care of ourselves, our family, and our colleagues at work.

MINDFUL SMILING

The next exercise is "Smile, release." "Breathing in, I smile; breathing out, I let go. Breathing in, I smile to my body; breathing out, I calm my body. Breathing in, I smile to my feelings; breathing out I calm my feelings. Smiling, releasing." Smiling is an effective practice. You don't need to feel one hundred percent joyful before you can smile, because smiling is a yoga practice. You practice yoga of the mouth. Even if you don't feel joyful, smiling helps relax the muscles on your face. There are about three hundred muscles on your face; when you're angry or fearful, these muscles get tense. If you look into a mirror at that moment, you see the tension on your face. But if you know how to breathe and smile, the tension will quickly fade, and you'll feel much better. You can help someone who is tense by smiling to her. She will feel much better after such a smile. "Breathing in, I smile. Breathing out, I let go of the tension."

Breathing in, you may be aware that you're angry about what another person said or did to you. Breathing out, you smile because you know that you're capable of embracing it and being at peace. Write this sentence on a piece of paper the size of a credit card and put it in your purse or wallet: "Although right now I am angry at my beloved, deep down I know I am capable of being peace." Then, when you're about to lose your self-control, take it out, read it, and begin to breathe in and out. It is essential that you act quickly before you cause damage to yourself and your beloved. So put the Buddha into your wallet. And when you need him, take out your wallet reminder, read it, and go back to the practice.

WONDERFUL MOMENT

The last exercise of the poem is: "Breathing in, I dwell in the present moment. Breathing out, I know it is a wonderful moment. Present moment, wonderful moment." We have learned that the only moment for us to be alive is the present moment. This is so even for inmates serving long prison sentences. When I gave a talk at the Maryland Correctional Facility near Washington, D.C., I told 150 prisoners that it's possible to be happy in the here and now. I told them, "When I walked into this prison, going through many, many metal gates, I noticed that the quality of the air inside is exactly the same as outside. The sky, looking from in here, is as blue as the sky outside, and the plants in the compound of the prison are as green as the grass outside. You have here all the conditions to practice mindful walking and mindful breathing. If you know how to practice, this very moment can be a wonderful moment. You don't need to be released from this place in order to be happy." The people in the prison listened attentively, and they were motivated to practice.

In any situation of difficulty that we find ourselves in, if we know how to open ourselves to the conditions for happiness and well-being that are always there, then the present moment will be a wonderful moment. Happiness is available in the here and now. It takes practice to be in the present moment. We need to practice in order to resist the tendency to run into the future or dwell on the past. We need to learn how to celebrate life in the present moment.

CALMING STRONG EMOTIONS

Many of us suffer from strong, painful emotions and don't know how to handle them. When you notice that there's a feeling in you that isn't calm or peaceful, you can repeat to yourself, "Breathing in, I am present for my feeling. Breathing out, I calm my feeling." When you say this, your emotion begins to calm down. This is important. The emotion may be despair, fear, or anger, but whatever it is, mindful breathing will calm it.

When you notice a strong emotion arising, go back to yourself and begin the practice of mindful breathing to generate the energy of mindfulness for your protection. Be there for your emotion and don't just let it overtake you. Don't become a victim of your emotions.

It's like when you know a heavy storm is coming. You have to do everything you can to protect your house so that it won't be damaged by the wind. Strong emotions come from within, from the depths of our consciousness. The energy of mindfulness also comes from the depths of our consciousness. So you sit in a stable position, in a chair with your feet flat on the floor or cross-legged on a cushion, or you lie down, and you prepare yourself for the emotion. You begin to breathe in and out, and you focus your attention on your abdomen. Why your abdomen? When you see a tree in a storm and you focus your attention on the top of the tree, you feel vulnerable. You have the impression that the tree is too fragile to withstand the storm, because the little branches and the leaves on the top of the tree sway violently in the wind. You have the impression that the tree will be blown away. But if you focus your attention on the trunk of the tree, you get a different impression. You can see that the tree is solid and rooted deeply in the soil, so you know the tree will withstand the storm.

You are also a tree, and that strong emotion is the storm that is approaching. If you don't prepare for it, you may be blown away. To prepare means to begin mindful breathing and to bring your attention down from the level of thinking to the level of the belly, just below the navel. This is called belly breathing. Just focus all your attention on your belly and become aware of the rise and fall of your abdomen, which is the trunk of your tree. Don't stay on the level of the brain because that is where the storm winds are blowing the hardest. It's dangerous to stay at the level of your thinking. Go down and embrace the trunk of the tree just below the navel, where you will be safe.

This is a simple practice, but it's effective. You're aware that an emotion is only an emotion. It's just a small part of your whole being. You are much more than your emotion. An emotion comes, stays for a while, and goes away, just like a storm. If you're aware of that, you won't be afraid of your emotions. Many young people don't know how to handle their emotions, and they suffer greatly. They believe the only way to end the suffering is to kill themselves. There are many young people who commit suicide simply because they don't know how to handle their emotions. Yet it's not difficult. It's helpful to know that an emotion is just an emotion, and that you are much more than your emotions, which come, stay awhile, and go. Why should you die because of an emotion?

When you focus your attention on your abdomen for fifteen or twenty minutes and take refuge in the practice, your emotion will subside. Then you'll feel peaceful and happy because you know there's a way to handle your emotions. You know that next time an emotion arises, you can do exactly the same thing.

When you've practiced and you have confidence in the practice, you can help someone who is close to you when they are overwhelmed by a strong emotion. You might say, "Come and sit by my side. Take my hand. Let us practice mindful breathing and pay attention to the rise and fall of our abdomens." Holding that person's hand, you can convey your strength and confidence. The two of you will be breathing in and out together. Fifteen or twenty minutes later, she will feel all right. In the future she can do it by herself. Teaching a friend how to practice like that may save her life later on.

I advise you not to wait until a strong emotion comes before beginning the practice. You'll surely forget to do it. Learn it right now. Practice fifteen minutes every day. Sit or lie in a stable position and practice mindful breathing. Enjoy your in-breath and your out-breath, and focus your attention on the abdomen. Belly breathing can be very deep, very slow, and very powerful. If you continue doing this for three weeks, you'll develop the right practice. Then, when a strong emotion arises, you'll remember the practice and you will succeed in soothing your emotion. Each time, your emotion becomes a little less powerful. You don't have to fight; you just allow the energy of mindfulness to embrace your emotion. Then it will weaken and go back to the depths of your consciousness.

TOTAL RELAXATION

People in any profession can profit from doing total relaxation every day or every week. Maybe there's a place in the office where you can practice total relaxation for fifteen minutes. You can do it at home also. Once you have benefited from practicing on your own to renew yourself, you can offer a session of total relaxation to your family or to your colleagues at work. You could have a session of total relaxation at your job every day. When co-workers and employees are overwhelmed by stress, they are much less effective in their work and often miss work because of sickness. This is costly for the organization, so fifteen minutes of total relaxation after three or four hours of work is practical. You may want to lead the total relaxation yourself. You will experience a lot of joy doing this. When you're able to make people happy and relaxed, your own happiness increases at the same time.

When we do deep relaxation in a group, one person can guide the exercise using the following instructions or some variation of them. You may want to sound a bell at the beginning and end of the exercise to help people more easily enter a relaxed state of mind. When you do deep relaxation on your own, you can use a recording to guide you.

Lie down on your back with arms at your sides. Make yourself comfortable. Allow your body to relax. Be aware of the floor underneath you ... and of the contact of your body with the floor. Allow your body to sink into the floor.

Become aware of your breathing, in and out. Be aware of your abdomen rising and falling as you breathe in and out ... rising ... falling ... rising ... falling.

Breathing in, breathing out.... Your whole body feels light ... like a water lily floating on the water.... You have nowhere to go ... nothing to do.... You are as free as the cloud floating in the sky.

Breathing in, bring your awareness to your eyes. Breathing out, allow your eyes to relax. Allow your eyes to sink back into your head.... Let go of the tension in

all the tiny muscles around your eyes.... Our eyes allow
us to see a paradise of forms and colors.... Allow your
eyes to rest.... Send love and gratitude to your eyes.

Breathing in, bring your awareness to your mouth.
Breathing out, allow your mouth to relax. Release the
tension around your mouth.... Your lips are the petals of
a flower.... Let a gentle smile bloom on your lips....
Smiling releases the tension in the hundreds of muscles
in your face.... Feel the tension release in your cheeks
... your jaw ... your throat.

Breathing in, bring your awareness to your shoulders.
Breathing out, allow your shoulders to relax. Let them
sink into the floor.... Let all the accumulated tension
flow into the floor.... We carry so much with our
shoulders.... Now let them relax as we care for our
shoulders.

Breathing in, become aware of your arms. Breathing
out, relax your arms. Let your arms sink into the floor ...
your upper arms ... your elbows   your lower arms ...
your wrists ... hands ... fingers ... all the tiny muscles....
Move your fingers a little if you need to, to help the
muscles relax.

Breathing in, bring your awareness to your heart.
Breathing out, allow your heart to relax. We have
neglected our hearts for a long time by the way we work,
eat, and deal with anxiety and stress. Our hearts beat for
us night and day. Embrace your heart with mindfulness
and tenderness, reconciling with and taking care of your
heart.

Breathing in, bring your awareness to your legs. Breathing out, allow your legs to relax. Release all the tension in your legs ... your thighs ... your knees ... your calves ... your ankles ... your feet ... your toes ... all the tiny muscles in your toes.... You may want to move your toes a little to help them relax.... Send your love and care to your toes.

Bring your awareness back to your breathing ... to your abdomen rising and falling.

Following your breathing, become aware of your arms and legs.... You may want to move them a little and stretch.

When you feel ready, slowly sit up. When you are ready, slowly stand up.

You can modify this short guided relaxation to suit your own particular needs. You can practice for just five minutes or as long as you wish. This exercise can guide awareness to any part of the body: the hair, brain, ears, neck, lungs, each of the internal organs, the digestive system, or to any part of the body that needs healing and attention. You embrace each part and send it your love, gratitude, and care as you hold it in your awareness and breathe in and out.

STRESS MANAGEMENT

It's not costly to set up a stress management program in your company or organization. It is important to train some assistants so they become skillful in the art of dealing with stress. These people have to practice for themselves first. They must be convinced of the benefit of total relaxation, mindful breathing, smiling, and walking to be effective in their task. Then they can share their practice with the other employees.

In Plum Village, we practice going back to our breathing and relaxing our body every time we hear a temple bell. In your company, you might like to do that too. You and your co-workers may select short sections from your favorite pieces of music—even just one minute long. Every hour or two, you play those short sections of music for the whole company over the public address system. When they hear this music, everyone stops what they are doing and becomes aware of their body, enjoying breathing and relaxing. Change the pieces of music regularly. You will see that after a month the atmosphere will change. The sound of the music functions like the voice of the Buddha within you, calling you back to smile, breathe, and renew yourself, or the voice of God calling you back to your true home.

ANSWERING THE TELEPHONE

In Plum Village, when the telephone rings, we stop whatever we are doing and return to our breathing. "Breathing in, I calm myself. Breathing out, I smile." We breathe in and out like this for three telephone rings before we pick up phone. That way, when we answer, we are calm and compassionate. The person on the other end will hear this in the quality of our voices.

When you touch the seeds of calm, solidity, and compassion in yourself, the quality of your conversations will improve.

Many of our friends practice telephone meditation at home and at work. Every time they hear the phone ringing, they stop and breathe mindfully. They enjoy their in-breath and their out-breath, and by doing so they become more calm, more peaceful; this has a very positive effect on their business. I know a businessman who always practices mindful breathing before answering phone calls, and he told me that it helps him become fully present on the call.

MINDFUL EATING

Eating mindfully is also a wonderful practice. While we eat, we focus our attention on just two things: we're aware of the food and aware of our environment. We don't think of the past, we don't think of the future, and we don't think of our projects and worries. We bring all our awareness to the food and the people around us. We practice eating in such a way that joy and happiness are possible while we eat. When we pick up a piece of food, we become aware of it. We look deeply into it to see that it is a gift from the sky, the earth, and much hard work. After looking at the piece of food, we put it into our mouth and chew it carefully, mindfully.

When I pick up a piece of carrot, I like to be with the carrot. It's like opening the door or lighting an incense stick. As I shared with you earlier, I was taught to invest one hundred percent of myself in closing the door or lighting an incense stick.

When I pick up a piece of carrot, I do the same. I use my body and mind to pick up the piece of carrot. I look at it to recognize it as a piece of carrot. If my mind was preoccupied with other things, like my project or the past or the future, I wouldn't know that I had put a piece of carrot in my mouth.

I invite you to eat mindfully. Before you put the carrot into your mouth, you might say its name silently: "Carrot." It's as if you are mindfully calling the name of your beloved, and the piece of carrot reveals herself to you clearly. When you put it into your mouth, you are aware that it is carrot you are putting in your mouth. As you chew the piece of carrot, you know that you are chewing your carrot and not your projects, your sorrow, your anger, the past, or the future.

You do only one thing at a time. When you pick up the piece of carrot in this way, you may have a deep insight about the carrot. You see all the elements that have made the carrot possible. You can see the clouds floating in the piece of carrot, you can see the sunshine, you can see the earth in the piece of carrot. In fact, the piece of carrot is a representative of the whole cosmos coming to you. And you can smile to it. It doesn't take a lot of time. Maybe one second is enough. If you are mindful and concentrated, you will attain insight into the true nature of the carrot.

In the Catholic Church, believers celebrate the Eucharist. The priest breaks the bread and offers it to you. He says that the bread is the body of Jesus Christ. If you know how to receive it, you will be purified and have eternal life. A piece of carrot is also the body of the cosmos coming to you, and if you know how to receive it, you are blessed with true life. But if you eat it in forgetfulness, the opposite of mindfulness, there is no life. When you are absorbed in your thinking, your sorrow, your ideas, your anger, the piece of carrot is no longer an ambassador of the cosmos.

In Plum Village we eat the first part of our meals in silence, because if we talk a lot we can't focus our attention on the food, and we won't be able to treasure the precious presence of our loved ones eating with us. When we eat together as a community, it is wonderful to stop eating from time to time and become aware of the people sitting and eating mindfully with us. Their presence is a support that helps us practice deeply. The silence can be powerful and eloquent. It can help us be there one hundred percent.

To help us savor the food, we can eat more slowly. It is beneficial to chew at least thirty times before we swallow each bite. While chewing, we breathe and relax, allowing ourselves to be in the here and now. Sometimes I chew my food with the help of the poem we used earlier: "In, out. Deep, slow." I chew my food while following my breath, and I feel happy in the here and now.

There are people who have introduced the practice of a silent, mindful lunch at their workplace. Their friends and co-workers eat quietly for ten or fifteen minutes before beginning to talk, and they enjoy it a great deal.

APPENDIX B

Work and Pleasure:
The Example of Patagonia

My experience of power, from the time I was very young, is that of a monk. I would like to share with you the story of someone who came to understand spiritual power through the world of business. Yvon Chouinard entered the business world in the 1950s, when he was a champion rock climber and began designing, manufacturing, and distributing rock-climbing equipment. In 1964, he produced a one-page mail-order catalog for a business he named Patagonia. The catalog advised people to expect very slow shipments during the rock-climbing season because he'd be out climbing. By the mid-1980s, his company was doing $20 million in sales, and by the mid-1990s it was doing $100 million.

Today, Patagonia has sales of more than $230 million annually. Yvon Chouinard is still the owner of the company, and he spends much of his time testing equipment around the world—hiking, kayaking, and climbing. *Fortune* and *Working Mother* magazines named Patagonia one of the hundred best companies in the country to work for. In 2004 Chouinard began an ocean initiative to support the health of the oceans. Patagonia has donated more than $22 million since 1985. In his book, *Let My People Go Surfing*, he talks about how Buddhism and mindfulness enhanced his business. "As it turns out," he writes, "the perfect place I found to apply Zen philosophy is in the business world."

Like Yvon Chouinard, each of us has, at least for an instant, experienced awakening: a moment of clarity, insight, and liberation. It may have come to you on a walk in the woods or on the beach, or in a quiet moment with a friend or a child. It may be a simple moment when you go back to yourself and drink a cup of tea mindfully: "Drinking my tea, I know that I am drinking tea." This is already awakening. You are awake to the fact that you are drinking tea and sitting with friends. If you continue to practice awakening, you'll have a greater awakening. You'll begin to figure out something that you hadn't been able to understand in the past, and you'll say, "Ah, I see." The highest awakening, which makes you a buddha, is made up of small awakenings that we all can realize in our daily life.

Awakening is not the business of bodhisattvas and buddhas alone. Awakening is everybody's business. With mindfulness and community, we can transform ourselves, those close to us, those in our work environment, and our workplace itself. We can be in the business of producing awakening every day—for our own sake, for our own well-being and happiness, and for the well-being and happiness of all living beings.

Here is Yvon Chouinard, in his own words, on how compassion and mindfulness can make our businesses a pleasure for ourselves, and a gift for our employees and for the world:

I've been a businessman for almost fifty years. It's as difficult for me to say those words as it is for someone to admit being an alcoholic or a lawyer. I've never respected the profession. It's business that has to take the majority of the blame for being the enemy of nature, for destroying native cultures, for taking from the poor and giving to the rich, and for poisoning the Earth with the effluent from its factories. Yet business can also produce food, cure disease, control population, employ people, and generally enrich our lives. And it can do these good things and make a profit without losing its soul.

I'm a very reluctant businessman. I'm a kid from the sixties and I rejected all of that stuff. And so because of that I feel a bit like a samurai businessman. If you wanted to be a samurai, you couldn't be afraid of dying, because if you flinch a little bit your head gets cut off. Since I never wanted to be a businessman, I could take a lot of risks and I could break a lot of rules because I didn't care whether I lost my business or not. That gave me a lot of freedom.

I took a trip to Scotland in the winter one year, and when I was there I bought a rugby shirt. This was around the mid-sixties, and at that time active sportswear for men was basically gray sweatshirts and sweatpants. Men didn't wear the colorful sportswear that they do now. But I had this rugby shirt with blue and red and yellow stripes. And I thought it made a great climbing shirt, because it had a collar and so your hardware slings didn't cut into your neck, and it was made out of real tough material. So I started wearing it climbing, and everybody would come up to me and say, "Wow, where'd you get that cool shirt?" So, you know, the entrepreneurial lightbulb came on in my head, I imported a few from England and they sold straightaway. So I got more, and pretty soon I started making shorts and ... that's how I got into the clothes business.

One day I saw my friend Doug Tompkins wearing a brushed wool pullover. And I thought, "Wow, that's pretty cool. If that could be made out of a synthetic, so it's more practical in the outdoors, it would be a great product. So my wife went down to the Cal Mart in L.A. where you buy fabric, looking for synthetic fleece. And she found some imitation fur stuff that they were selling for people to use for toilet seat covers. It was this awful looking stuff. But we made a jacket out of it, and it worked. It really worked great. You could fall into a river in the winter, take it off and shake it and all the water would run out, and put it back on and it would save your life. We gradually improved the product, until the mid-eighties, when we came out with a really nice-looking fleece product. It wasn't just functional, it actually looked good too. And we called it "synchilla."

Suddenly our business took off, because everybody wanted to buy synchilla. So we were selling the stuff to everybody. And we were growing the business fifty percent a year, we were opening up lots of wholesale accounts, we were opening up our own retail stores, we were sending our catalogs to mailing lists, to people who didn't request it, but we were sending them the catalog anyway. We got caught in this trap of growth, never really thinking of what we were doing—this growth was coming to us and we were accepting it. In 1989, we had planned to do another fifty percent increase in business, we had hired one hundred new people to support all that growth, we'd bought all the inventory. And a recession hit. We only grew twenty percent. You know, it doesn't sound like bad growth, twenty percent, but when you're ramped up to do fifty, it's a disaster. And at the same time our bank was in financial trouble, so they were calling in their loans. So as you can imagine with an estimated fifty percent growth every year, we had some real cash flow problems in the beginning. I was desperate for loans. My accountant even introduced me to some Mafia connections who wanted to loan me some money for twenty-eight percent interest—which is, ironically, what you have to pay with credit cards these days. Anyway, it was a real crisis for us; we almost lost the company. And I realized that my company was unsustainable.

Right in the middle of the crisis, I took ten of our most important people, and we took a walkabout down into Patagonia—the real Patagonia, in South America. We'd walk around for a half hour or so in the wilderness, then we'd all sit down in a circle and we'd talk about, "What are we doing here anyway? Why are we in business?" None of us had wanted to be businesspeople—not one of us had a degree in business—and yet we were. And so we started talking about what our values were.

And the first one that came up was quality. We really took pride in making the best climbing equipment in the world. Not "among the best," but the very best. And so it was important to us to also do that with clothing. We really were committed to making the absolute best, and we were committed to putting all the principles of industrial design into designing those clothes. We wanted to make really functional, hard-wearing, yet good-looking clothing. My designer at the time said, "Well, we can't make the best clothes in the world." I said, "Well, why not?" He said, "Well, the best shirt is made of hand-woven Italian fabric, the buttons are hand-sewn, it's a Giorgio Armani one-of-a-kind shirt and they cost $300.00." I said, "Well what happens if you take that shirt and you throw it in the washing machine?" "Oh, you can't do that; it'll shrink." And I said, "Well, that's not good quality." We were our own customers, and I knew that we wanted to wash that shirt in a bucket or a sink or the edge of a stream and have it dry and put it on in a couple of hours and get on the airplane. So we had to identify what we meant by quality. And there were no books on what is quality in clothing. We had to figure out our own criteria for quality.

Something else we really valued was flex time. When I had a partner in the climbing equipment business, he'd take off to do an expedition to Annapurna in the Himalayas and he'd be gone for four or five months and I'd run the business. And then he'd come back and I'd take off, drive down to the tip of South America from California and climb for six months, and he would watch over the business. That's why my book is called *Let My People Go Surfing*. We have a company policy that says: you go surfing when the surf comes up. Pretty simple, isn't it? But you know what? Most people go surfing next Tuesday at two o'clock, because that's when they have time off. You need to stay home to take care of your kids when they're sick. It's a different attitude. If you're a really serious surfer, you make sure you have a job, you have a life that allows you to go surfing when the surf comes up.

The other thing we wanted to do is blur the distinction between work and play and family. We wanted to continue making stuff that we used. We wanted to have our families with us. We didn't want to disappear for eight hours a day. So in the beginning, we had new mothers with their babies in cardboard boxes on their desk. That worked a little bit for a while. We have open offices—we don't have any cubicles, it's all open offices—so that contributes to really good communication. But one time somebody had a baby that was a screamer and that became a real problem. The mother had to go out and sit in her car with this kid that was screaming like crazy. So my wife said, "I've had it, we're going to start a child-care center." We started one of the first on-site corporate child-care centers in America. That's ethics, and it's just good business. Eighty percent of my employees were women. I didn't want to lose them. They say when you have to replace an employee it costs you $50,000, it's much better not to lose a good employee.

The other thing we wanted to do is we wanted to continue hiring friends. No one in my company had an MBA. Everybody had a degree in anthropology, biology, sociology or, like me, had a degree from John Burroughs High School in auto mechanics. We always had an attitude that instead of hiring people who studied business in school, we'd much rather hire passionate people who'd be interesting to go to dinner with and who did the sports that we were making stuff for. And then we'd teach them business. We'd all learn business together, because we didn't know what the heck we were doing. It's much better than hiring a businessperson and trying to get them passionate about kayaking or climbing or something.

We wanted to make the best stuff. We wanted to go to work with friends, surrounded by friends. We wanted to work on the balls of our feet and have our families with us. On that trip to Patagonia, I took those values and started writing them down and they gradually turned into a philosophy of doing business. When I got back, we had to lay off twenty percent of our workforce in order to save the business. It was the hardest thing I ever had to do because these were friends; and I swore that I would never ever go through that situation again. And so we decided to really try to be a more sustainable business.

About the same time, I started getting really concerned about environmental degradation around the planet. We had a mission statement that said: "Make the best quality product." That was our mission statement. So I added one more part to the mission statement: "Cause no unnecessary harm." It didn't say "cause no harm," because that's stupid, there's no way you can make a product, manufacture anything without causing harm. There's no such thing as perfect sustainability. There's a beginning and end to everything, there's a limit to every resource. But we wanted to minimize that; it's a matter of degrees.

I also started taking fifteen of our employees at a time, and we'd spend five days talking about the different philosophies of business. "What are we trying to do in retail? What's our philosophy of retail? What's our philosophy of architecture?" I mean, do we go into malls and be next to Sees Chocolates? Or do we try to find old buildings somewhere and restore them and make it a gift to the neighborhood? I did that with every single employee in the company and that got us all aligned in one direction. I had a psychologist do a study of all our employees one time. He said to me, "You know, this is really strange, I've got to tell you this. I've looked at all your employees here, and I've never seen such independent people. In fact they are so independent, they are unemployable in other companies." That was music to my ears. When you have all those independent people, the only way you can lead them is with consensus. They have to be convinced that it's the right thing to do. And that's what I was doing with this "philosophy class."

I've always thought a responsible farmer leaves the land in better condition than it was in when he received it; a forester leaves the forest in better condition, he doesn't just clear-cut it; and a responsible government makes its decisions as if the society is going to be here, like the Iroquois say, for seven generations into the future—they don't make these little short-term decisions. But somehow, business is exempt from all of that. Business can grow as fast as it possibly can. The sole mandate of a CEO of a public corporation is to maximize profits for the shareholders. I decided to try to run my business as if it's going to be here one hundred years from now, and so we made all our decisions from then on according to that. It means that, even if you grow ten or fifteen percent a year, in twenty or thirty years you're a multi-trillion dollar company—which is impossible, of course. But that's what everybody else is trying to do. We put our business on a rate of growth that was sustainable. From that time on, we've thrived. We got out of debt, because I didn't trust the banks. We grew through what we called "natural growth." We don't encourage artificial growth by, for example, advertising in urban areas so that people buy our clothes as status symbols and not because they're actually planning on using them for outdoor activities. That's not sustainable. In fact, the reason I got in trouble in the first place is that I started selling to people who wanted those fleece jackets but didn't need them. So whenever you're making products for people who want but don't really need them, you're at the mercy of the economy, and I didn't like that at all.

The other little mindful lesson I learned is that profits happen when you do everything right. And so even though some years we have three percent growth, we still make a profit, because my company is set up to be profitable with three percent growth. Most companies, unless they're growing ten percent or more, are not profitable. It's just a matter of how you set the company up. If you ask me what our profits were last year, or what they're going to be this year, I have no idea, I couldn't tell you. I have no interest in it, for one thing. I just know that the process is going well, and at the end of the year we will be profitable.

The last part of our mission that I had to write up was our environmental philosophy. That was the most difficult to write. It's basically a five-step philosophy.

1. Lead an Examined Life

I firmly believe that most of the damage caused to the planet is caused unwittingly. It's caused by ignorance, by people who just don't ask enough questions. You know, there's a method of management at Toyota that says when you have a problem, you ask "why" five different ways, you ask five different questions, before you try and figure out an answer. Unfortunately most of society and certainly the government, we don't ask enough questions. That's why we end up working on symptoms all the time; we don't really work on the causes. For instance, one out of eight women in the United States is going to get breast cancer. Before World War II it was about one in thirty or forty, but now it's one in eight. It's not all genetics. Yet all the organizations working on cancer are working on cures. Only three percent of the monies that go to breast cancer research go to finding causes of breast cancer. There are 300,000 toxic chemicals in use today, any one of which, or some combination, could cause breast cancer. But our general society's philosophy is we're not going to get rid of those chemicals, so let's find a cure. The traditional thinking is that there's no money to be made in finding causes, there's only money to be made in cures.

To lead an examined life—let's say you want to feed your family healthy food. You have to know where it comes from. You can't just go to Safeway and buy some tomatoes, because they may have come from Mexico, a country that still uses DDT. You have to know the farmer and you have to ask a lot of questions. We didn't know what we were doing in making clothing. We had no idea. We'd just call up a fabric supplier and say, "Hey, give us 10,000 yards of shirting in this color or this pattern," and that was it. We started asking the question, "Okay, of all the fibers used in making clothing, which ones are the most toxic, and which ones are the most benign?" It's not easy to find the answers to that. But after digging around a lot, we finally found out that the most damaging fiber to be making clothing out of, by far, was one hundred percent cotton. Cotton uses twenty-five percent of the world's pesticides and it only occupies three percent of the world's farmland. To pick the cotton with mechanical pickers, you have to defoliate the plant and you use paraquat for that, the same stuff we sprayed on Vietnam. All of those chemicals go into the aquifer, as well as into the workers' lungs. The cancer rate in cotton-growing areas is ten times above the normal. I went to the Central Valley and started looking at some cotton fields, and I was aghast. It was a killing zone out there. There's nothing alive. No weeds, no birds, no insects. There's nothing. It's just dead. And there are big sumps out there, big lakes, where the water comes up from all that irrigation and all those chemicals. They have to hire people to sit on lawn chairs with cannons and shotguns so that when the waterfowl come to land on the water, they scare them away, because if the birds get some of that water in them they'll have chicks with two beaks and three legs.

I came back and I said, "Okay, we're getting out of the cotton business. I will not be part of that." It's like you're a little company making land mines, and you're one of the best companies to work for in America and you're hiring people, giving them a job—but you're making land mines. And you go to Cambodia and all of a sudden you see the results of your work. Now you have a choice: you can either continue making land mines with guilt, or you get out of the business.

I gave the company eighteen months to completely stop using any industrially grown cotton. Thankfully, there's an alternative. I didn't have to get out of the cotton business, because there was organically grown cotton. But, I don't just call a fabric supplier and say, "Hey, you know that shirting I ordered? Switch to organically grown." It wasn't that easy. We had to work with the gins and the mills and the spinners and find non-toxic dyes, and it was really hard, but it mobilized the whole company. And we learned finally how to make clothing. The other thing is, when you buy cotton clothing, only seventy-three percent of that shirt or that pair of pants is actually cotton, even though it says one hundred percent cotton. The other is all chemicals put on the fabric, and formaldehyde is one of the most common, and it's to make that cotton stay pressed and not shrink. So it actually makes a more practical product, putting all those chemicals on. But we weren't about to use organically grown cotton and put all the chemicals on it—and toxic chemicals as well. So we had to learn how to do it by construction. You know, maybe use a longer staple cotton and spin it a little tighter, pre-shrink it. So we had to learn how to make clothes. That was all the result of asking one question.

2. Clean Up Your Own Act

Leading an examined life in business is a real pain, let me tell you. It adds a complexity that most businessmen don't want to deal with, they don't want to hear about this stuff. But after you've educated yourself, you find out what you're doing, then you have to act. And that's the second step, which is to clean up your own act. It doesn't matter whether you're a businessman or you're an individual. The Zen master would say: If you want to change government, don't focus on changing government; you're not going to get anywhere. You've got to change the corporations, because government's just a pawn of the corporations. Well, if you want to change corporations, you've got to change consumers. That's where the buck stops, with us. We are the consumers. We're not citizens anymore, we're consumers. We're the ones that feed the corporations that feed the government. So we're the ones that have to change. So once you find out that you're the one, that we're part of the problem, then finally you can be part of the solution.

One of my favorite quotes is from Thoreau. He said, "Beware of any endeavor that requires new clothes." Do you need yoga pants to do yoga? That's kind of silly as far as I'm concerned. My attitude is: consume less, but consume better. The Europeans only consume twenty-five percent as much as we do; but when they buy a coat or a jacket or a pair of pants, they buy the best quality they can and they keep it for a long time. They're not just consuming, discarding, consuming, discarding—that's why we're in the hole we're in. So that's what I'm trying to do with my own business. We're trying to question every process, every material we use, educate ourselves, and then act on it.

3. Do What You Can Do

Since we can never be a completely sustainable company and we can never make a completely sustainable product, the third step is to do what we can. In this day and age, if you're a good speaker, you've got to speak out. If you're a good writer, you've got to write. You've got to volunteer for organizations. We have to do something, because if we just sit back and be complacent, say like many Germans were during Hitler's reign, you're going to lose your soul. So we all have to do something.

Being the owner of a company that employs 1,100 people, and being pretty visible, I feel I have a responsibility to use my company to do some good. We dig into our pockets. We take one percent of our sales and we give that away to environmental causes. The reason we give to environmental causes is, I think practically every problem we have in society can be traced back to an environmental cause. Whether it's poverty, or crime, it's an estrangement from nature, whatever it is.

4. Support Civil Democracy

The fourth step is to support civil democracy. Of all the powerful forces in America, from federal government to state government to local government to religion or whatever you want to name, the most powerful force of all is civil democracy. If you open up the newspaper on any day of the year, you'll see that every gain we're making as a society is being made by activists. If you look at the history of America, look at the Boston Tea Party: you know it's a bunch of activists who dropped the tea in the Boston Harbor. The Civil War—you think, Lincoln freed the slaves. Well, the slaves were being encouraged to flee the South by the Underground Railroad, which was being funded by Northern philanthropists. They were leaving at such a rate that the South was freaking out. Lincoln just wanted to keep the country together. If you look at civil rights—it wasn't the government that enacted civil rights legislation, it was Rosa Parks, a middle-aged black woman who just didn't want to get off the bus. It was a bunch of Black kids who didn't want to go to segregated schools. That's who enacted civil rights. Vietnam—we got out of Vietnam because of activism. The government didn't want to get out of Vietnam. People say Teddy Roosevelt established Yosemite National Park. It wasn't Teddy Roosevelt, it was John Muir who encouraged Teddy Roosevelt to go camping with him and go sleep under the redwoods and ditch the Secret Service and got Roosevelt all fired up and then he went back and designated it a national park; but John Muir was the man. Women's suffrage ... you know, if we ever get out of Iraq, it's going to be because of activism. So that's what we do with our one percent.

5. Be a Role Model

The last part of our five steps is to influence other companies, influence other people. We're not going to save the world by ourselves. So we have to lead other people into doing the right thing. And the only way to lead is by example. That's the only way. If I had a business that did all the right things but didn't make a profit, I wouldn't get the business world to respect me at all. They'd say, "Ah, those guys can do that, but they don't make a profit." So I have to be profitable. I have to act just like a regular business. I can't be a pseudo-environmental organization. Our people who do environmental assessment and ask all those questions are in contact with lots of other companies and we're sharing information, and when one company finds a better way to make something or a better process that is less harmful, we share that information together.

The proudest thing I've done is, I've started an organization called "One Percent for the Planet" which is now an alliance with 224 other companies that are all pledged to give one percent of their sales to environmental causes. Each company gives to the organizations of their choice. We don't give their money away; there's just a small charge to belong to the organization. We only check to see that they give the money away. It's just very small companies. I've found that when a company gets to be medium-size or so they get kind of tight with their money. Almost all the charity given away in America is given away by individuals. Corporations only give away three percent of all the philanthropy. It seems like the richer you get, the less money you give away. So there are barbershops, and mountain guides, and vineyards, and one of the most notable members is Jack Johnson, the singer. You'll see that One Percent for the Planet logo on the back of his CDs. A lot of people think: "Great, Patagonia gives all this money away, so, okay, when I get rich, I'm going to start giving some money away too." But, you know what, if you're a true capitalist, you're going to understand that $10 given away today is going to do a lot more good than $100 given away ten years from now, because that $10 starts working right now, and it just accumulates and gets more and more valuable. So think about that.

The last part of our mission statement is to use business to inspire and implement solutions to the environmental crisis. For me, that's the main reason I'm in business right now. I never wanted to be a businessman, but I guess I am one, and I guess I probably will be one for a long time. But that's the reason I'm in business.

Thich Nhat Hanh has retreat communities in southwestern France (Plum Village), New York (Blue Cliff Monastery), and California (Deer Park Monastery), where monks, nuns, laymen, and laywomen practice the art of mindful living. Visitors are invited to join the practice for at least one week. For information, please write to:

Plum Village
13 Martineau
33580 Dieulivol
France
NH-office@plumvillage.org (for women)
LH-office@plumvillage.org (for women)
UH-office@plumvillage.org (for men)
www.plumvillage.org

For information about our monasteries, mindfulness practice centers, and retreats in the United States, please contact:

Blue Cliff Monastery
3 Hotel Road
Pine Bush, New York 12566
Tel: (845) 733-4959
www.bluecliffmonastery.org

Deer Park Monastery
2499 Melru Lane
Escondido, CA 92026
Tel: (760) 291-1003
Fax: (760) 291-1172
www.deerparkmonastery.org
deerpark@plumvillage.org